A Retreat With
Jessica Powers

Loving a Passionate God

Robert F. Morneau

St. Anthony Messenger Press
Cincinnati, Ohio

Other titles in the
A Retreat With... *Series:*

Cover illustration by Steve Erspamer, S.M.
Cover and book design by Mary Alfieri

ISBN 0-86716-236-8

Published by St. Anthony Messenger Press
Printed in the U.S.A.

Contents

Introducing A Retreat With...

Twenty years ago I made a weekend retreat at a Franciscan house on the coast of New Hampshire. The retreat director's opening talk was as lively as a long-range weather forecast. He told us how completely God loves each one of us—without benefit of lively anecdotes or fresh insights.

As the friar rambled on, my inner critic kept up a sotto voce commentary: "I've heard all this before." "Wish he'd say something new that I could chew on." "That poor man really doesn't have much to say." Ever hungry for manna yet untasted, I devalued any experience of hearing the same old thing.

After a good night's sleep, I awoke feeling as peaceful as a traveler who has at last arrived safely home. I walked across the room toward the closet. On the way I passed the sink with its small framed mirror on the wall above. Something caught my eye like an unexpected presence. I turned, saw the reflection in the mirror and said aloud, "No wonder he loves me!"

This involuntary affirmation stunned me. What or whom had I seen in the mirror? When I looked again, it was "just me," an ordinary person with a lower-than-average reservoir of self-esteem. But I knew that in the initial vision I had seen God-in-me breaking through like a sudden sunrise.

At that moment I knew what it meant to be made in the divine image. I understood right down to my size eleven feet what it meant to be loved exactly as I was. Only later did I connect this revelation with one granted to the Trappist monk-writer Thomas Merton. As he reports in *Conjectures of a Guilty Bystander*, while standing all unsuspecting on a street corner one day, he was overwhelmed by the "joy of being...a member of a race in which God Himself became incarnate.... There is no way of telling people that they are all walking around shining like the sun."

As an absentminded homemaker may leave a wedding ring on the kitchen windowsill, so I have often mislaid this precious conviction. But I have never forgotten that particular retreat. It persuaded me that the Spirit rushes in where it will. Not even a boring director or a judgmental retreatant can withstand the "violent wind" that "fills the entire house" where we dwell in expectation (see Acts 2:2).

So why deny ourselves any opportunity to come aside awhile and rest on holy ground? Why not withdraw from the daily web that keeps us muddled and wound? Wordsworth's complaint is ours as well: "The world is too much with us." There is no flu shot to protect us from infection by the skepticism of the media, the greed of commerce, the alienating influence of technology. We need retreats as the deer needs the running stream.

An Invitation

This book and its companions in the *A Retreat With...* series from St. Anthony Messenger Press are designed to meet that need. They are an invitation to choose as director some of the most powerful, appealing and wise mentors our faith tradition has to offer.

Our directors come from many countries, historical

eras and schools of spirituality. At times they are teamed to sing in close harmony (for example, Francis de Sales, Jane de Chantal and Aelred of Rievaulx on spiritual friendship). Others are paired to kindle an illuminating fire from the friction of their differing views (such as Augustine of Hippo and Mary Magdalene on human sexuality). All have been chosen because, in their humanness and their holiness, they can help us grow in self-knowledge, discernment of God's will and maturity in the Spirit.

Inviting us into relationship with these saints and holy ones are inspired authors from today's world, women and men whose creative gifts open our windows to the Spirit's flow. As a motto for the authors of our series, we have borrowed the advice of Dom Frederick Dunne to the young Thomas Merton. Upon joining the Trappist monks, Merton wanted to sacrifice his writing activities lest they interfere with his contemplative vocation. Dom Frederick wisely advised, "Keep on writing books that make people love the spiritual life."

That is our motto. Our purpose is to foster (or strengthen) friendships between readers and retreat directors—friendships that feed the soul with wisdom, past and present. Like the scribe "trained for the kingdom of heaven," each author brings forth from his or her storeroom "what is new and what is old" (Matthew 13:52).

The Format

The pattern for each *A Retreat With...* remains the same; readers of one will be in familiar territory when they move on to the next. Each book is organized as a seven-session retreat that readers may adapt to their own schedules or to the needs of a group.

Day One begins with an anecdotal introduction called "Getting to Know Our Directors." Readers are given a telling glimpse of the guides with whom they will be sharing the retreat experience. A second section, "Placing Our Directors in Context," will enable retreatants to see the guides in their own historical, geographical, cultural and spiritual settings.

Having made the human link between seeker and guide, the authors go on to "Introducing Our Retreat Theme." This section clarifies how the guide(s) are especially suited to explore the theme and how the retreatant's spirituality can be nourished by it.

After an original "Opening Prayer" to breathe life into the day's reflection, the author, speaking with and through the mentor(s), will begin to spin out the theme. While focusing on the guide's own words and experience, the author may also draw on Scripture, tradition, literature, art, music, psychology or contemporary events to illuminate the path.

Each day's session is followed by reflection questions designed to challenge, affirm and guide the reader in integrating the theme into daily life. A "Closing Prayer" brings the session full circle and provides a spark of inspiration for the reader to harbor until the next session.

Days Two through Six begin with "Coming Together in the Spirit" and follow a format similar to Day One. Day Seven weaves the entire retreat together, encourages a continuation of the mentoring relationship and concludes with "Deepening Your Acquaintance," an envoi to live the theme by God's grace, the director(s)' guidance and the retreatant's discernment. A closing section of Resources serves as a larder from which readers may draw enriching books, videos, cassettes and films.

We hope readers will experience at least one of those

memorable "No wonder God loves me!" moments. And we hope that they will have "talked back" to the mentors, as good friends are wont to do.

A case in point: There was once a famous preacher who always drew a capacity crowd to the cathedral. Whenever he spoke, an eccentric old woman sat in the front pew directly beneath the pulpit. She took every opportunity to mumble complaints and contradictions—just loud enough for the preacher to catch the drift that he was not as wonderful as he was reputed to be. Others seated down front glowered at the woman and tried to shush her. But she went right on needling the preacher to her heart's content.

When the old woman died, the congregation was astounded at the depth and sincerity of the preacher's grief. Asked why he was so bereft, he responded, "Now who will help me to grow?"

All of our mentors in *A Retreat With...* are worthy guides. Yet none would seek retreatants who simply said, "Where you lead, I will follow. You're the expert." In truth, our directors provide only half the retreat's content. Readers themselves will generate the other half.

As general editor for the retreat series, I pray that readers will, by their questions, comments, doubts and decision-making, fertilize the seeds our mentors have planted.

And may the Spirit of God rush in to give the growth.

Gloria Hutchinson
Series Editor
Conversion of Saint Paul, 1995

Getting to Know Our Director

In the summer of 1983 someone asked me if I knew a poet by the name of Jessica Powers. The name rang no bell. I was then gifted with a small volume of verse entitled *The House at Rest*, published privately by the Carmelite Monastery in Pewaukee, Wisconsin, the residence of Sister Miriam of the Holy Spirit, who published under her baptismal name, Jessica Powers. The book contained sixty-four poems, many of which spoke directly to my heart. I knew that I must someday meet this insightful woman.

Later that summer I called the Carmelite Monastery in Pewaukee in the hope of making an appointment to see Sister Miriam of the Holy Spirit. The call was successful: I could stop by for a visit the first week of September.

That introduction, that gift of verse and the later meeting with Jessica Powers deeply influenced my life. I now take this opportunity to introduce you to a woman who loved God, who hungered for holiness, who suffered under the shadow of the cross, who knew how to laugh and sigh and love. She gifted the world by sharing many of her experiences through poetry.

On my drive to the monastery, questions swirled through my mind. Who is this Carmelite nun who has been writing poetry for over fifty years? What does she look like? How did she acquire such a creative gift of wrapping words around the deepest longings of the human heart? Would she be affable or retiring?

Any apprehensions beneath these questions were unfounded. I was soon to meet a humble, witty fellow creature less than five feet tall and then in her late seventies. I encountered a person who centered her life on the mystery of God. We sat and talked for nearly an hour.

My stereotypes of people in contemplative life were once again dismantled. Jessica Powers was both serious and joyful. She told of her love for community and Saint John of the Cross; she spoke of poets who shaped and touched her life; she sang of her love for the Church and expressed deep concern for the suffering people of the world.

I asked if she had poems other than the ones I had read in *The House at Rest*. Too late I realized the foolishness of the question. She gently informed me that she had written well over four hundred poems, possibly more. I inquired further: Are these accessible? Yes, many had been published over the years in various periodicals.

I learned that Sister Regina Siegfried from St. Louis had been gathering Jessica's poetry together over the years. But Jessica clearly stated that much of her early poetry was not of publishable quality. Our conversation drifted into what makes a good poem, how poetry reflects faith, the great poets of history.

In that first encounter I met someone who was deeply embedded in the human condition. Here was someone who did not run away from her humanity but was willing to struggle with life in all its complexity and ambiguity. Here was someone who would make good company on a retreat because her poetry presents all the large questions we must deal with on life's journey: Who are we? Who is God? What is at the heart of reality? How do we get back home?

I left the Carmelite Monastery that day knowing that I

would return often to share concerns, to receive inspiration, to talk about poetry and life. Now I invite you to do the same, to make a retreat with Jessica Powers by prayerfully pondering her verse. It may be a dangerous journey because both poetry and prayer are transformative.

Three vignettes: While living in New York in the late 1930's, before her entrance into the Carmelite community in 1941, Jessica Powers was having a discussion with an editor when the conversation turned theological. What was the greatest attribute in God, truth or beauty? As Jessica Powers narrates the story, she held out for beauty as the deepest revelation of God, whereas the editor sided with truth. The dialogue went on for over two hours with no discernible victory.

Years later, in relating this "argument," Jessica Powers laughed and said: "We were both wrong. God's greatest attribute is mercy. In the end, that's all we have and should desire."

To know Jessica Powers is to know someone who lived a God-centered life. Her response to a contemplative calling gave outer expression to an interior summons. For forty-seven years she lived in the cloister, journeying with her sisters (and the larger Church) in a life of prayer, penance and witness. This Godward existence governed her heart. She knew the Center; she also knew the periphery of struggle and darkness. Her trust in a God of mercy and truth and beauty sustained her all her life.

A second story: In the early 1920's Jessica was doing secretarial work in Chicago. Though there were times of loneliness, she valued the rich cultural opportunities and the possibility of establishing strong friendships. Then her mother died. Jessica, at no small sacrifice, returned to her rural homestead near Mauston, Wisconsin, to tend to the needs of her two bachelor brothers.

She witnessed to sacrificial self-giving, a central gospel value, in this return home. She remained there for eleven years, doing domestic work, setting aside her personal dreams and desires. This characteristic, forgetting self in tending to the needs of others, would continue throughout her life. People had primacy over her personal ambitions.

A third snapshot: A month before her death, Jessica sat through an extensive session, going through all of her poetry with Sister Regina Siegfried and me. Our task was to choose from some four hundred poems those writings which would go into a selected edition. Though ill and weak, Jessica demonstrated the qualities that characterized much of her life: humility, humor and a hunger for God.

Artists, like all gifted persons, are subject to pride. How easy it is to think that a talent is of one's own making. Jessica Powers knew that her gift came from God, was nurtured by God and grew through grace. I sensed even a certain level of embarrassment as she attached her name at the end of a poem.

Jessica Powers was a private person. Although we had some deep exchanges during my numerous visits with her, she would be adamant now that I not focus on her or our relationship in this retreat. Her desire was that her poetry would reveal what her life was all about—the mystery of God, not herself. To be with Jessica Powers is to be with and in her poetry. In this retreat she speaks in the poems she chose for *Selected Poetry of Jessica Powers*.

A humble artist almost prefers anonymity since one is "only" a conduit for Truth and Beauty to become incarnate in our world. In 1947 Jessica articulated her understanding of humility:

Humility

Humility is to be still
under the weathers of God's will.

It is to have no hurt surprise
when morning's ruddy promise dies,

when wind and drought destroy, or sweet
spring rains apostatize in sleet,

or when the mind and month remark
a superfluity of dark.

It is to have no troubled care
for human weathers anywhere.

And yet it is to take the good
with the warm hands of gratitude.

Humility is to have place
deep in the secret of God's face

where one can know, past all surmise,
that God's great will alone is wise,

where one is loved, where one can trust
a strength not circumscribed by dust.

It is to have a place to hide
when all is hurricane outside.

Humility gives one a sense of proportion which in turn
culminates in humor. Jessica's Scottish-Irish wit was
observable in the twinkle of her eye, in stories of mishaps
and pranks, in lines from her poetry. In "But Not With
Wine," God gets the blame for the soul's inordinate mirth
and indecorum because of "too much giving." Below the
warm smile and ready laughter there was a deep
seriousness, a tinge of melancholy. Jessica would not be

put off by humor or the lightness of being. She wanted to know, she wanted to love, she sought union with God and all creation.

Baron Von Hugel, the noted spiritual writer, held that religion is a "metaphysical thirst." Jessica Powers had a "metaphysical hunger" for God. By entering the Carmelite community she made herself fully accessible to God's comings. This life of prayer and penance in community with others became the environment for encountering the divine. No other food or drink would bring satisfaction. God was her Absolute, Jesus was her utmost need, the Spirit was, as Saint John of the Cross said, the "South Wind" of love and warmth. The temptations of life—power and pleasure, possessions and prestige—met in her heart a triune God and found no lodging. Jessica Powers responded to the invitation to be poor like Jesus, to become a disciplined beggar.

The Master Beggar

Worse than the poorest mendicant alive,
the pencil man, the blind man with his breath
of music shaming all who do not give,
are You to me, Jesus of Nazareth.

Must You take up Your post on every block
of every street? Do I have no release?
Is there no room of earth that I can lock
to Your sad face, Your pitiful whisper "Please"?

I seek the counters of time's gleaming store
but make no purchases, for You are there.
How can I waste one coin while you implore
with tear-soiled cheeks and dark blood-matted hair?

And when I offer You in charity
pennies minted by love, still, still You stand

fixing Your sorrowful wide eyes on me.
Must all my purse be emptied in Your hand?

Jesus, my beggar, what would You have of me?
Father and mother? the lover I longed to know?
The child I would have cherished tenderly?
Even the blood that through my heart's valves flow?

I too would be a beggar. Long tormented,
I dream to grant You all and stand apart
with You on some bleak corner, tear-frequented,
and trouble mankind for its human heart.

Placing Our Director in Context

Jessica Powers' geographic journey was fairly simple.
Except for one year at Marquette University in
Milwaukee and a year of secretarial work in Chicago, she
spent her first thirty-one years in rural Wisconsin on a
farm near Mauston. She was baptized on February 7,
1905, and confirmed in 1919 at St. Patrick's, the local
Catholic church. At age eleven she first experienced the
mystery of death when her seventeen-year-old sister
Dorothy died of tuberculosis. Two years later, in 1918,
her father died of a heart attack; her mother's death
occurred in 1925.

An early influence in Jessica's life was Dominican
Sister Lucille Massart, who encouraged her student to
write. A second major influence was the faith of her
Scotch-Irish heritage. Religion was in the air; God was a
felt presence. A third influence was nature, the haunting
beauty of the rural landscape and the strong seasons of
Wisconsin: spring meadows "where only the children
find the flowers";[1] summers in which "Deer had been

sighted near, the neighbors said, / so we were watching
when we saw them go / lightly through the field where
hazel brush had spread";[2] autumn's caution that "You are
a guest yourself and you must know / that in you lie the
instincts of migration, and where the bird went, one day
you will go";[3] and the winter chickadee "who makes the
weed of a December day / the pivot of his mirth."[4]

The next geographic place was New York (1936-1941).
During these years Jessica Powers came to treasure the
friendship of the Anton Pegis family. Anton, a
philosopher of note, his wife, Jessica (a poet in her own
right), and their two children became part of Jessica's
extended family. Jessica was nourished by stimulating
table conversation, by sharing verse with a companion-
poet, by the play and simplicity of children.

In the Catholic Poetry Society of America Jessica
shared her writings and received helpful critiques. Add
access to libraries, reading John of the Cross, the
friendship of editors, and one senses tremendous growth
in a young woman from a limited rural milieu. These
were rich and rewarding years.

Beneath the excitement and enrichment a call was
resounding. With no small sacrifice a decision was in the
making: Leave behind these friendships and
opportunities for creative exchange and come apart.
Abraham of old was indeed her father.

Abraham

I love Abraham, that old weather-beaten
unwavering nomad; when God called to him
no tender hand wedged time into his stay.
His faith erupted him into a way
far-off and strange. How many miles are there
from Ur to Haran? Where does Canaan lie,

or slow mysterious Egypt sit and wait?
How could he think his ancient thigh would bear
nations, or how consent that Isaac die,
with never an outcry nor an anguished prayer?
I think, alas, how I manipulate
dates and decisions, pull apart the dark,
dally with doubts here and with counsel there,
take out old maps and stare.
Was there a call at all, my fears remark.
I cry out: Abraham, old nomad you,
are you my father? Come to me in pity.
Mine is a far and lonely journey, too.

How can I summarize forty-seven years of religious life?
The cloister conceals contemplative knowledge and
protects privacy. Many things are simply matters of
history: Jessica's 1941 entry into the Carmel of the Mother
of God on Wells Street in Milwaukee; her first profession
on May 8, 1945, and perpetual profession a year later.
Elected prioress in 1955, she directed the 1958 move of
the Carmel from downtown Milwaukee to Pewaukee.
Jessica served two later terms as prioress and spent a year
in a tuberculosis sanatorium. She suffered a severe stroke
on August 17, 1988, and died the next day at the age of
eighty-three.

During these years the Second World War raged; the
Second Vatican Council met; technology revolutionized
the world. And in the cloister Jessica (now known as
Sister Miriam of the Holy Spirit) and her community
turned night and day to God in prayer and penance and
service. During these years friendships were forged,
poems were written, tears were shed, laughter enriched
evening meals. During these years the garden produced
yet another harvest, the geese called from their lofty
altitudes the song of adventure, winter and spring

brought sorrow and joy. Jessica remained faithful through the light and the dark.

Her life was limited geographically, but few people have ventured so far into the interior of the soul as she. There she found God as "a thousand acres,"[5] the strangest of all lovers,[6] the joy of the soul. In the end she found a God of mercy and salvation.

A word about poetry: Reading a poem is more like chewing a mouthful of steak than swallowing a spoonful of jello. If we gulp it down, its full nutritive value escapes us and we are still hungry. William Carlos Wiliams, himself a poet, once wrote: "It is difficult to get the news from poems./Yet [people] die miserably every day/For lack of what is found there." The poems of Jessica Powers are layered with good news. To "get it," we have to give ourselves to them, read them aloud, ponder their images and symbols, pray them with a grateful heart. As W.H. Auden said, every poem, from whatever pen, must do one essential thing: "praise all it can for being and for happening."

With this, I invite you to receive some Godward direction from a Carmelite sister, a Wisconsin poet, a rural farm girl who fell in love with a passionate God.

Notes

1 "A Meadow Moreover."

2 "Deer in the Open."

3 "For a Silent Poet."

4 "Look at the Chickadee."

5 "The Ledge of Light."

6 "God Is a Strange Lover."

DAY ONE
Loving a Creating God

Introducing Our Retreat Theme

There is essentially only one possible theme for a retreat with Jessica Powers: the mystery of a passionate God. She herself made the decision that the collection of her selected poetry should begin and end with the following two poems that center on the tremendous mystery of God's love:

The Mercy of God

I am copying down in a book from my heart's
    archives
the day that I ceased to fear God with a shadowy fear.
Would you name it the day that I measured my
    column of virtue
and sighted through windows of merit a crown that
    was near?
Ah, no, it was rather the day I began to see truly
that I came forth from nothing and ever toward
    nothingness tend,
that the works of my hands are a foolishness wrought
    in the presence
of the worthiest king in a kingdom that never shall
    end.

I rose up from the acres of self that I tended
   with passion
and defended with flurries of pride;
I walked out of myself and went into the woods of
   God's mercy,
and here I abide.
There is greenness and calmness and coolness, a soft
   leafy covering
from the judgment of sun overhead,
and the hush of His peace, and the moss of His mercy
   to tread.
I have naught but my will seeking God; even love
   burning in me
is a fragment of infinite loving and never my own.
And I fear God no more; I go forward to wander
   forever
in a wilderness made of His infinite mercy alone.

Doxology

God fills my being to the brim
with floods of His immensity.
I drown within a drop of Him
whose sea-bed is infinity.

The Father's will is everywhere
for chart and chance His precept keep.
There are no beaches to His care
nor cliffs to pluck from His deep.

The Son is never far away from me
for presence is what love compels.
Divinely and incarnately
He draws me where His mercy dwells.

And lo, myself am the abode

of Love, the third of the Triune,
the primal surge and sweep of God
and my eternal claimant soon!

Praise to the Father and the Son
and to the Spirit! May I be,
O Water, Wave and Tide in One,
Thine animate doxology.

Pondering the mystery of a passionate God may seem
rather theological, abstract, even esoteric. Such is not the
case. It is most pragmatic. Since we are made to the image
and likeness of God, to know God's essence is to come to
know ourselves and what life is all about. Spiritual
direction leads us to worship—to respond with love,
adoration and thanksgiving to who God is and what God
has done. Another aim of spiritual direction is to come to
know who we are and what we are called to do. Prayerful
reflection on the mystery of God moves us to the
achievement of this goal.

Jessica Powers provides us with a number of gerunds
(verbal nouns) that capture various aspects of God's life
and activity. Seven of these words offer a sevenfold
structure for our prayer, our purification, our call to
action. Here is the listing of various attributes of God to
be considered in our seven-day retreat: creating,
sustaining, calling, redeeming, challenging, delighting,
commissioning.

In this first session we plumb the mystery of a creating
God.

Opening Prayer

O creating and loving God,

we stand in awe at the marvels of your world:
    the vastness and beauty of the sea,
    the majesty and splendor of the mountains,
    the secrets of deserts and forests,
    the scent of clover, a patch of blue sky.

We kneel in reverence at the foot of the cross,
    where your creative love
    found full expression in Jesus.
As we begin this day of prayer
    send us your Spirit
    that we may feel your creative touch,
    be thankful for the gift of life
    and commit ourselves to praise and thanksgiving.

Lord, may we respond to your call
    to be creative life-givers
    in a world filled with violence and fear.

We ask all this through Christ our Lord. Amen.

RETREAT SESSION ONE

The Passion of a Creating God

Before we begin, take a moment to discover the wonder of your own created being.

Listen to your heartbeat; feel your pulse. Experience the gift of life here and now.

Become aware of your breathing. Be thankful for your existence.

Ask for the grace of reverence—a holy respect for God's creative love.

Our Creator God is the source of all life, all holiness.
Creation is not a mystery of the past; creation is
happening here and now. For those who are awake, for
those who exercise sensitivity and sensibility, the
response is one of praise and thanksgiving. All is gift; all
is grace; all, an expression of divine love.

Our spiritual director, Jessica Powers, appreciated
God's creative love. In her poem "For a Lover of Nature,"
this contemplative Carmelite invites you to watch the
Creator behold creation, to encounter the Love that
underlies life.

For a Lover of Nature

Your valley trails its beauty through your poems,
the kindly woods, the wide majestic river.
Earth is your god—or goddess, you declare,
mindful of what good time must one day give her
of all you have. Water and rocks and trees
hold primal words born out of Genesis.

But Love is older than these.

You lay your hand upon the permanence
of green-embroidered land and miss the truth
that you are trusting your immortal spirit
to earth's sad inexperience and youth.
Centuries made this soil; this rock was lifted
out of the aeons; time could never trace
a path to water's birth or air's inception,
and so, you say, these be your godly grace.
Earth was swept into being with the light—
dear earth, you argue, who will soon be winning
your flesh and bones by a most ancient right.

But Love had no beginning.

The deist would have us believe that God creates but then leaves the world to provide for itself. By contrast, belief in a providential Creator posits that every sparrow, every hair on our head, every moment of time has significance and value in God's sight. The theology of God's providence faces many difficulties because of the problems of suffering and evil. Yet a deep, accepting faith allows us to trust that when all is said and done, all will be well.

During a summer visit to her monastery, Jessica Powers took me on a tour of the property. With reverence she spoke of the beauty of the flowers, the melodies of the birds, the vastness of the sky. She was at home in creation; she was in love with the Creator.

Throughout her entire life she had a deep affection for the land. The meadows of western Wisconsin took her breath away; the stars in the evening sky turned her mind to the mystery of infinity. As she described some of her gardening duties I could tell that her heart was always captured by that which is beautiful. She loved colors, purples and lavenders and splashes of yellow. She loved the shades of blue, whether in summer weather or wintertime. Her eyes sparkled as they gazed about God's tremendous grandeur.

Jessica Powers invites us to see what she saw, how everything in creation is in a Godward movement. God's creative energy not only endows beings with existence, but that same energy draws us forward to our eternal destiny. The poet herself entered the race (this race in which all are to win the prize) and reminds us that we are invited to join in with the rest of creation on the journey home. For unlike trees and beetles and eels, humans have the option of thwarting the Godward life and exiting from the race.

As Jessica speaks in the following poems, walk with

this Carmelite nun who so loved the mystery of creation. Keep vigil with her and let your heart and soul sing the praises of God.

Now prayerfully ponder this prayer poem:

Everything Rushes, Rushes

The brisk blue morning whisked in with a thought:
everything in creation rushes, rushes
toward God—tall trees, small bushes,
quick birds and fish, the beetles, round as naught,

eels in the water, deer on forest floor,
what sits in trees, what burrows underground,
what wriggles to declare life must abound,
and we, the spearhead that run on before,

and lesser things to which life cannot come:
our work, our words that move toward the
    Unmoved,
whatever can be touched, used, handled, loved—
all, all are rushing on *ad terminum*.

So I, with eager voice and news-flushed face,
cry to those caught in comas, stupors, sleeping:
come, everything is running
        flying,
        leaping,
hurtling through time!
        And we are in this race.

For Reflection

- *Who are your companions in the race we call life?*

- *Someone said that spirituality is essentially a matter of staying awake. Do you suffer from "comas and stupors"?*

- *Do you feel a certain urgency ("rushes, rushes") to respond to the Godward life?*

- *What works and words of yours are truly creative and further God's creative designs?*

- *Do you have an "eager voice" in inviting others to join in the race toward heaven?*

A central ingredient on the spiritual journey is our image of God. The question of who God is shapes our self-understanding since, as believers, we know that we are made to God's image and likeness. To know who God is means to know who we are. Conversely, ignorance of God means lack of self-knowledge.

In spiritual direction the question arises as to the nature of God. For some the emphasis will be theocentric, focusing on God as the Absolute, the Holy Other. Another emphasis is Christocentric, with the mystery of the incarnation, redemption and resurrection playing a central role in our reflection on the divinity. Still others find the Holy Spirit at the core of their spiritual journey, a Spirit that enlightens and enkindles and enables individuals in community to realize their dignity and their destiny.

Whatever the focus, the mystery of the triune God will always involve creative, life-giving love. Spirituality is about life, life designed to be lived to the full (see John 10:10). A retreat gives each of us an opportunity to examine the quality of our existence: our reverence for our bodiliness, our psychological dispositions, our social and political involvements, our response to the daily stirrings of our God. Fullness of life is the invitation that awaits us every dawn.

Creation is a vast mystery. The poet Gerard Manley Hopkins calls us to a fundamental imperative: "Look at the stars!"[1] Looking with the eyes of faith opens for us a vision of God's glorious handiwork. The work reveals the worker; the portrait tells something about the heart of the artist; creation discloses attributes of the Creator. And, of course, we ourselves are part of God's creative design.

Ponder for a few moments these reflections of Jessica Powers as she describes her experience of the mystery of creation:

> Acres we are to be gathered for God: He would pour out His measureless morning
> upon divinized lands, bought by blood, to their Purchaser given.
> Oh, hear Him within you speaking this infinite love,
> moving like some divine and audible leaven,
> lifting the sky of the soul with expansions of light,
> shaping new heights and new depths,
> and, at your stir of assent,
> spreading the mountains with flame, filling the hollows with heaven.[2]

For Reflection

- *How does God speak "this infinite love" within you?*

- *In what ways does God's creative work depend upon our "stir of assent"?*

- *How does this poetic passage relate to the image of God the potter in Jeremiah 18:1-11?*

Closing Prayer

Poets offer an important perspective on life. Jessica Powers has given us some stunning insights into creation. But she kept expanding her vision through both prayer and study. God's word was central to her spiritual life, as were the teachings of the Church and the writings of significant authors.

To broaden our appreciation of the mystery of creation, to have yet another resource to deepen our prayer, here are selections from John's Gospel, the Second Vatican Council, the new *Catechism* and a contemporary writer. Feel free to use them or not as prayer-starters, as the Spirit moves you. Each quotation is introduced with a focusing question or statement.

God's Word. *Ask for the grace to hear these words as if for the first time; ponder them with reverence and awe.*

> In the beginning, when God created the heavens and the earth, the earth was a formless void and darkness covered the face of the deep, while a wind from God swept over face of the waters. Then God said, "Let there be light"; and there was light. And God saw that the light was good; and God separated the light from the darkness. God called the light Day, and the darkness he called Night. And there was evening and there was morning, the first day. (Genesis 1:1-5)

The Second Vatican Council. *What is your sense of dependency upon the Lord? Pray for "poverty of spirit."*

> But if the expression "the independence of temporal affairs" is taken to mean that created things do not depend on God, and that humanity can use them

without reference to their Creator, anyone who acknowledges God will see how false such a meaning is. For without the Creator the creature would disappear. For their part, however, all believers of whatever religion have always heard God's revealing voice in the discourse of creatures. When God is forgotten, the creature itself grows unintelligible. (*Pastoral Constitution on the Church in the Modern World*, #36)

Catechism of the Catholic Church. Retreat is a time to revisit the large questions of life. Prayerfully ask for the gift of wisdom.

Catechesis on creation is of major importance. It concerns the very foundation of human and Christian life: for it makes explicit the response of the Christian faith to the basic question that men of all times have asked themselves (Cf. *Declaration on the Relation of the Church to Non-Christian Religions*, #2): "Where do we come from?" "Where are we going?" "What is our origin?" "What is our end?" "Where does everything that exists come from and where is it going?" The two questions, the first about origin and the second about the end, are inseparable. They are decisive for the meaning and orientation of our life and actions. (#282)

Contemporary Writing. *What is the quality of your fidelity, of your obedience to the gift of life? What does existence mean to you?*

But creation is a call to be in a continuing relation with the caller. Existence therefore means to be continually answering the caller in new forms of fidelity and obedience. Our life is not for self-indulgence nor for desperate coping, nor for frantic, empty surviving. It is life lived after the manner of this very God who empties himself to obedience in the life of Jesus.[3]

Notes

[1] "The Starlit Night," *Poems of Gerard Manley Hopkins*, edited by W.H. Gardner (New York and London: Oxford University Press, 1948), p. 27.

[2] "This Is a Beautiful Time."

[3] Walter Bruggemann, *The Bible Makes Sense* (Winona, Minn.: St. Mary's Press, 1977), p. 22.

DAY TWO
Loving a Sustaining God

Coming Together in the Spirit

Jessica Powers died on August 18, 1988. Several months before her death, she spent some time in a local hospital. I had the opportunity of visiting with her as she experienced the mystery of suffering. Though her body was weak and fragile, her faith was strong.

My memories are clouded by time and space. Yet certain images are clear. One is the cross that was always present in Carmelite spirituality, the cross that Jessica wore. It was this Christian symbol that spoke to her of God's providence. Jessica knew that God was with her in her pain, in the diminishment of her body. She knew that despite physical and spiritual loss, God was providential. Her eyes spoke hope, her words hidden in her heart.

One confirmation of God's sustaining providence came for Jessica in the care of her community. She loved and cared for her sisters, as they did for her. Providence for Jessica was not an ethereal reality. It was as real as a phone call, the delivery of mail, the daily visits of her sisters.

Defining Our Thematic Context

Jessica Powers experienced God as Sustainer. In fact, God had taken up residence in her heart. Two years before entering the Carmel our spiritual director wrote:

The Kingdom of God

Not towards the stars, O beautiful naked runner,
not on the hills of the moon after a wild white deer,
seek not to discover afar the unspeakable wisdom,—
the quarry is here.

Beauty holds court within,—
a slim young virgin in a dim shadowy place.
Music is only the echo of her voice,
and earth is only a mirror for her face.

Not in the quiet arms, O sorrowful lover;
O fugitive, not in the dark on a pillow of breast;
hunt not under the lighted leaves for God,—
here is the sacred Guest.

There is a Tenant here.
Come home, roamer of earth, to this room and find
a timeless Heart under your own heart beating,
a Bird of beauty singing under your mind.

Opening Prayer

Providential and loving God,
    may your concern,
    your abiding presence and friendship
    be felt daily in our hearts.

Our planet is often dark,
    darkened by a greed that blinds us,

darkened by violence that destroys our sensitivity.
Your light does shine in the darkness.
Help us to see your graciousness
  in the warmth of the sun,
  the consolation of the wind,
  the cleansing of the rain,
  the nourishment of the earth.

May we take nothing for granted
but be filled with gratitude, indeed, praise.
Send your Spirit
  to help us know your ongoing love;
send Jesus into our hearts
  to help us know
  that Bethlehem and Calvary happen yet again.

Gracious God, we thank and praise you.

RETREAT SESSION TWO

The Passion of a Sustaining God

Jessica Powers lived in rural western Wisconsin. Often the winter storms would sweep in from the west, making roads impassable, closing schools. When the snows were wet and heavy, every tree (except the mighty oaks) was endangered—especially the evergreens, whose broad branches caught every flake that fell. If the wind did not blow away the gathering accumulation, many a tree broke.

By analogy, a similar experience happens in the human soul. The snows of worry, anxiety and suffering pile high, and limits can be reached. Does God care? Will

God intervene? Is the faith claim of providence for real?

Listen now as Jessica sings of God's faithful providence.

The Cedar Tree

In the beginning, in the unbeginning
of endlessness and of eternity,
God saw this tree.
He saw these cedar branches bending low
under the full exhaustion of the snow.
And since He set no wind of day to rising,
this burden of beauty and this burden of cold,
(whether the wood breaks or the branches hold)
must be of His devising.

There is a cedar similarly decked
deep in the winter of my intellect
under the snow, the snow,
the scales of light its limitations tell.

I clasp this thought: from all eternity
God who is good looked down upon this tree
white in the weighted air,
and of another cedar reckoned well.
He knew how much each tree, each twig could bear.
He counted every snowflake as it fell.

For Reflection

- *Take a good look at an evergreen. Imagine it weighted with wet, heavy snow. Recall a time in your life when you were weighed down by joy or sorrow. Did you hold or break? Why?*

- *Ask for the grace of confidence and trust in God's devising.*

32

- *Are the hairs on your head counted—by you, your beautician or barber, by God? Some think not. Take the musical* Show Boat *and listen to the haunting song "Old Man River." The words and melody leave us hopeless. If the river (read God) knows something, it "don't say nothin'." The philosophy articulated here is one of massive indifference—or, more kindly, benign neglect.*

- *By contrast, our faith tells us that God is deeply concerned about every moment of life. Prayerfully listen to these Gospel words:*

> [Jesus] said to his disciples: "Therefore I tell you, do not worry about your life, what you will eat, or about your body, what you will wear. For life is more than food, and the body more than clothing. Consider the ravens: they neither sow nor reap, they have neither storehouse nor barn, and yet God feeds them. Of how much more value are you than the birds! And can any of you by worrying add a single hour to your span of life? If then you are not able to do so small a thing as that, why do you worry about the rest?" (Luke 12:22-26)

This call to trusting faith bumps up against some hard history: the incredible Holocaust, the massacre of the innocent, the tragic suffering of AIDS patients. We are forced on retreat to face evil and suffering; we are forced to deal with the ancient question of a good God and massive cruelty in the world. The question: Does God care? Does God support and sustain us in our daily lives? Or are we forever locked into a certain "homelessness" and loneliness?

> It is the homelessness of the soul in the body sown;
> it is the loneliness of mystery:
> of seeing oneself a leaf, inexplicable and unknown,
> cast from an unimaginable tree;
> of knowing one's life to be a brief wind blown
> down a fissure of time in the rock of eternity.[1]

These are real questions that try the heart. It's one thing to believe that our God is Creator; it's another matter to claim that God's providence is a reality. Yesterday we spent time looking into the mystery of life and praying about the origin of all that is. Even many contemporary scientists are open to the element of mystery: "Can we really hope to answer the ultimate questions of existence through science and rational inquiry, or will we always encounter impenetrable mystery at some stage?"[2] But to create a universe and then walk away is one thing (read deism). To create and sustain expresses a fuller life, a deeper commitment, a covenant indeed. Jessica Powers believed in providence. She also wrote about that belief and invites us into the mystery.

Saint John of the Cross maintains that when God looks, God loves. So when God sees cedar trees and refugees, when God perceives a soul struggling between the gravity of sin and the grace of goodness, when God beholds the vastness of the galaxies and the shortness of time—God loves. Jessica Powers knew well the writings of John of the Cross. His theology strengthened her faith. Thus, God counted every snowflake that settles in the soul. And God cared.

There is a strange denial today in the lives of many of us. If God sees and cares, then there should be no suffering. Is it possible that God sets no wind arising to scatter the pain that comes our way? Is it possible that part of the divine devising is that we bear the burden of beauty, the burden of coldness?

The burden of illness bends low the branches of those with terminal cancer. What is one's philosophy of life, what is one's theology in such circumstances? Listen reverently to the "vision statement" of someone dying of a brain tumor who continues to believe in providence:

> I guess I could make a little Vision Statement now. I'm recording this on May 8, 1994, and I have been given a death sentence by the doctors that I probably will not live too long, certainly not a year, they tell me. But I do have a vision.... It's a vision of simple kindness, of love that is extended to one another in perfect simplicity. It is a vision today that this is good enough for the good God, that he takes tremendous delight in our simple acts of love for one another.
>
> I feel life right now with such simplicity I never dreamed that it was possible. I see part of the vision as letting go of rules and regulations that hinder the freedom of spirit that God wants us to have in our relations with one another. I see the vision as we are a community that is bound together in love, opening ourselves to others in simple, tiny acts of love, even though they may seem to us no more than a drop in the ocean, and with faith so full and trusting that we know that even in the simple drop, God can do marvelous and beautiful things in the souls that can change lives and transform the world.... And we say to people: God is good, and you're good, and life is good. And it's enough for God. Don't tie yourself up in knots. Don't kill the Spirit by too much programming. Just love, try your best to love, as much as you can, every day, and it's enough for God. Our good and simple God is truly good.[3]

Retreat is a time to clasp and clarify certain thoughts, as Jessica Powers did: "I clasp this thought: from all eternity / God who is good looked down upon this tree / white in the weighted air, / and of another cedar reckoned well. / He knew how much each tree, each twig could bear. / He counted every snowflake as it fell."[4]

Some thoughts to clasp:

> Bear one another's burdens.... (Galatians 6:2a)

> I am the vine, you are the branches. (John 15:5a)

> I came that they may have life, and have it
> abundantly. (John 10:10b)

Is it possible in your life to sketch out a vision statement? Each of us has an implicit philosophy; it is good at times to make it explicit. This helps us to stay focused and centered as our modern culture shouts multiple messages in our ears. If our faith is strong, part of our vision will record how God journeys with us.

Faith in God's providence assures us that together we celebrate the days when the travel is light; together we share the burdens that weight the soul.

Ponder for a few moments these reflections of Jessica Powers as she describes her experience of the mystery of divine providence:

> Down in the valley there was such a stir:
> A sparrow reached the sun!
> Why had the wind and weather favored her?
> What had she ever done?
> Yet since they must, they spoke the praising word,
> measured her flight and paused to gasp afresh.
> What was she really but a little bird,

all feather and no flesh?
Only the sun knew, and the moving air
the miracle thereof:
a bird that wings itself with resolute love
can travel anywhere.[5]

For Reflection

- *When has God's wind and weather favored you?*

- *Is your love resolute? How do you know?*

- *How do you "provide" and "support" God? Is there such a thing as reverse providence?*

Closing Prayer

Jessica Powers meditated on the Gospels. Sit with her as together you ponder the lilies of the fields and God's providential love. Join Jessica in deciphering the signs of the times and how faith illumines God's presence in the world. Reflect on God's guidance of nature and history, a God who gives us rest. And pause to experience that at this present moment we are being sustained by God's power and presence.

God's Word. *What is your level of trust in God's providence? Ask for the deepening of the gift of faith.*

> Consider the lilies, how they grow: they neither toil nor spin; yet I tell you, even Solomon in all his glory was not clothed like one of these. But if God so clothes the grass of the field, which is alive today and tomorrow is thrown into the oven, how much

more will he clothe you—you of little faith! And do not keep striving for what you are to eat and what you are to drink, and do not keep worrying. For it is the nations of the world that strive after all these things, and your Father knows that you need them. Instead, strive for his kingdom, and these things will be given to you as well. (Luke 12:27-31)

Vatican Council II. *What are the signs of God's presence in your life? Does your faith cast a light on all things?*

The People of God believes that it is led by the Spirit of the Lord, who fills the earth. Motivated by this faith, it labors to decipher authentic signs of God's presence and purpose in the happenings, needs and desires in which this people has a part along with others of our age. For faith throws a new light on everything, manifests God's design for humanity's total vocation, and thus directs the mind to solutions which are fully human. (*Pastoral Constitution on the Church in the Modern World*, #11)

Catechism of the Catholic Church. *In the face of evil and sin, how do you sustain trust in divine providence?*

We firmly believe that God is master of the world and of its history. But the ways of his providence are often unknown to us. Only at the end, when our partial knowledge ceases, when we see God "face to face" (1 Corinthians 13:12), will we fully know the ways by which—even through the dramas of evil and sin—God has guided his creation to that definitive sabbath rest (Cf. Genesis 2:2) for which he created heaven and earth. (#314)

Contemporary Writing. *What is God's will for you?*

Again and again Jesus speaks of his Father's will.
This paternal will is not to be understood as a fixed,
preconceived program including everything that
will ever occur in the course of time. Rather, it lives,
takes shape in Jesus, directing him during the
progress of events according to the need of the hour.
The Father and his will are with him always,
upholding, surrounding, fulfilling and urging him
constantly on.[6]

Notes

[1] "There Is a Homelessness."

[2] Paul Davies, *The Mind of God: The Scientific Basis for a Rational World*
(New York: Simon & Schuster, 1992), p. 20.

[3] Sister Anita Marie Cervenka, "The Vision Is Pressing to Its Time,"
ND Connection (newsletter of the Sisters of Notre Dame of
Chardon, Ohio), June/July 1994, Vol. X, No. IX.

[4] "The Cedar Tree."

[5] "The Legend of the Sparrow."

[6] Romano Guardini, *The Lord* (Chicago: Henry Regnery Company,
1954), p. 34.

Day Three
Loving a Calling God

Coming Together in the Spirit

The God of Scripture creates and sustains all of life.
We do well to pause on our journey and keep vigil at
these mysteries. For the gift of life we give thanks; for
God's sustaining providence we offer praise.

But spiritual amnesia is a problem for many of us. We
forget from whence we came; we take for granted the
daily blessings that nourish our physical, psychological
and spiritual lives. Forgetting God endangers the quality
of our faith and leads to a sense of being lost. Retreat is a
time to refocus on the mysteries of life, how God
continues to be with and for us—and to call us.

Opening Prayer

God of Abraham and Sarah,
God of Mary and Joseph,
    open our ears to the sound of your voice,
    our eyes to the splendor of your plan.
You call us to lives of holiness and service.
Grant us your Spirit of charity and generosity,
    that we may further your kingdom
    by doing your will.
Heal our deafness and cowardice.

Form us into the image of Jesus,
your Son and our Lord. Amen.

RETREAT SESSION THREE

The Passion of a Calling God

Moses, Abraham and Saint Paul each heard a call at strange times and in diverse places: before a burning bush, on a sacrificial mountain, along a murderous road. They heard a passionate voice and made a response. God continues to call today. God calls each of us by name and issues a particular task. Vocation, not job or career, characterizes the journey of a believer.

Jessica Powers was a good listener. When God called to her heart, she responded. As a contemplative, she tells us in the following poem, she felt God's call in these terms: "Come to me here in this secret place."

This Is a Beautiful Time

This is a beautiful time, this last age, the age of
the Holy Spirit.
This is the long-awaited day of His reign in our
souls through grace.
He is crying to every soul that is walled:
Open to Me, My spouse, My sister.
And once inside, He is calling again:
Come to Me here in this secret place.
Oh, hear Him tonight crying all over the world
a last desperate summons of love to a dying race.

Acres we are to be gathered for God: He would pour

out His measureless morning
upon divinized lands, bought by blood, to their
Purchaser given.
Oh, hear Him within you speaking this infinite love,
moving like some divine and audible leaven,
lifting the sky of the soul with expansions of light,
shaping new heights and new depths,
and, at your stir of assent,
spreading the mountains with flame, filling the
hollows with heaven.

For Reflection

- *How many telephone callers can you identify simply by the sound of their voice?*

- *List the times you have heard God's call.*

- *Ask for the grace of freedom so that, when the call comes, you will be free to go.*

While in New York in the late 1930's, Jessica Powers fell in love with the writings of Saint John of the Cross, the great Carmelite mystic. While I was visiting one day she told me: "When I first read Saint John of the Cross, I thought I had died and gone to heaven."

Jessica Powers knew that God calls us in many ways. Not infrequently our vocation is actuated by the experience of others, those who have discerned the voice of God and responded in deep ways. Jessica Powers' fondness for the writings of John of the Cross lay in the fact that this mystic centered upon the mystery of God.

Even though the journey to God's mountain involved dark nights and gray days, nothing was to prevent the climb, nothing to prevent the total self-giving to the Lord.

On our retreat with Jessica Powers we are the beneficiaries of her experience. She passes on to her readers the insights of the mystics; she gives us in poetic form her experience and her interpretation of the search for mystical union. The images of dark night, of silent music, of the mountain, of purification disclose how the classical writers assisted her in responding to God's call. Our vocation, our calling, can be deepened as we pray along with this Carmelite tradition. We take yet another step on our faith journey. It is a step similar to that taken by the prophet Jeremiah. Listen to the story of how God breaks into his life:

> Now the word of the LORD came to me saying,
> "Before I formed you in the womb I knew you,
> and before you were born I consecrated you;
> I appointed you a prophet to the nations."
> Then I said, "Ah, Lord GOD! Truly I do not know
> how to speak, for I am only a boy." But the LORD said
> to me,
> "Do not say, 'I am only a boy';
> for you shall go to all to whom I send you,
> and you shall speak whatever I command you,
> Do not be afraid of them,
> for I am with you to deliver you,
> says the LORD."
> Then the LORD put out his hand and touched my
> mouth; and the LORD said to me,
> "Now I have put my words into your mouth.
> See, today I appoint you over nations and over
> kingdoms,
> to pluck up and to pull down,
> to destroy and to overthrow,

to build and to plant." (Jeremiah 1:4-10)

Of course, Jeremiah's story is our own. Before he was called, God knew and consecrated him. It is clear that God formed Jeremiah in his mother's womb and sustained him after birth. Now the call comes. Not surprisingly, the initial response is one of resistance. Who of us wants to leave our comfort zones? Who wants to live in the unknown and not be in control? Who wants to go to strange lands and speak what another commands?

God calls! God has given each of us a vocation, a task to accomplish on this earth. Even small children know this:

> I don't want to waste my time here on this earth....
> When you're put here, it's for a reason. The Lord wants you to do something. If you don't know what, then you've got to try hard to find out what. It may take time. You may make mistakes. But if you pray, He'll lead you to your direction. He won't hand you a piece of paper with a map on it, no sir. He'll whisper something, and at first you may not even hear, but if you have trust in Him and you keep turning to Him, it will be all right.[1]

Jessica Powers wrote some of her poems from a passing comment or a verse that touched her heart. She once heard Father Mary Barnabas Ahern state: "Virtue it is that puts a house at rest." She was also familiar with the poetry of John of the Cross. Using the metaphor of a house being at rest, she wrote the following poem, a poem which can serve as a context for praying over our own call and the degree of our personal freedom.

The House at Rest

On a dark night
Kindled in love with yearnings—
Oh, happy chance!—
I went forth unobserved,
My house being now at rest.—Saint John of the Cross

How does one hush one's house,
each proud possessive wall, each sighing rafter,
the rooms made restless with remembered laughter
or wounding echoes, the permissive doors,
the stairs that vacillate from up to down,
windows that bring in color and event
from countryside or town,
oppressive ceilings and complaining floors?

The house must first of all accept the night.
Let it erase the walls and their display,
impoverish the rooms till they are filled
with humble silences; let clocks be stilled
and all the selfish urgencies of day.

Midnight is not the time to greet a guest,
Caution the doors against both foes and friends,
and try to make the windows understand
their unimportance when the daylight ends.
Persuade the stairs to patience, and deny
the passages their aimless to and fro.
Virtue it is that puts a house at rest.
How well repaid that tenant is, how blest
who, when the call is heard,
is free to take his kindled heart and go.

Three conditions for prayer are silence, solitude and surrender. Such dispositions are not easily come by in our noisy, activist, controlling culture. But we cannot hear

God or others unless we hush our houses. It is good in retreat to take inventory and note carefully those factors which do not allow silence to find a home within us. A partial list is sufficient to indicate a major problem: complaining ceilings, vacillating stairs, so many events banging on our doors and windows. Is it any surprise that the whispers of God are difficult to comprehend?

Further, silence needs some solitude. There are seasons and times in our life that exclude both foes and friends. We need to be alone with the "Alone." Community is important and often mediates grace, clarifying for us the Lord's purposes. But community without some solitude can quickly become superficial if not erroneous in its work of discernment. Midnight is a good time to pull the shades, invite the stairs to rest and wait upon the voice of the Lord.

God's call will always involve some aspect of love. Our universal vocation, according to Vatican II, is holiness, the perfection of charity.[2] Thus, happiness lies in freely responding to God's call when it is heard. This is what we call surrender, another name for abandonment. The poet Virgil reminds us that in God's will is our peace.

In Jessica Powers's poem entitled "Abraham," the same theme arises (see page 14). After reflecting on Abraham's deep faith, the poet turns upon herself (and every reader) with the confronting query: "Was there a call at all, my fears remark." So easily we dally with doubt, take out old maps, become confused by diverse counsel. God's voice and plan are obscured by the clutter of our hearts and the clatter of our minds.

For Reflection

- *Read Luke 1:26-38. What enabled Mary to respond to God's call?*

- *What enables you to respond to God's call?*

- *What are some signs that help you to know that you are responding to God's voice and not to your own ego?*

- *Is your prayer a dialogue or a monologue?*

Closing Prayer

Find a quiet place and reread slowly the poem "The House at Rest" (see page 46). Then enter into dialogue with Jessica Powers as you ponder these parallel readings. The following questions might arise: Where did James and John get the freedom to say yes to the Lord? What is the difference between God's call to religious life in contrast to the vocation of the laity? What are the various ways in which our vocation is handed on to future generations? Is the poet's way different from that of other people? Is our vocation ultimately all the same: to be pilgrims and exiles? What does our experience say to these questions? What does the poetry of Jessica Powers have to say?

God's Word. *When did God first call to your heart? What fishing boat were you in at the time?*

> As [Jesus] walked by the Sea of Galilee, he saw two brothers, Simon, who is called Peter, and Andrew his brother, casting a net into the sea—for they were fishermen. And he said to them, "Follow me, and I will make you fish for people." Immediately they

left their nets and followed him. As he went from
there, he saw two other brothers, James, son of
Zebedee and his brother John, in their boat with
their father Zebedee, mending their nets, and he
called them. Immediately they left the boat and their
father, and followed him. (Matthew 4:18-22)

Vatican Council II. *What is your understanding of vocation?*

But the laity, by their very vocation, seek the
kingdom of God by engaging in temporal affairs
and by ordering them according to the plan of God.
They live in the world, that is, in each and in all of
the secular professions and occupations. They live
in the ordinary circumstances of family and social
life, from which the very web of their existence is
woven. They are called there by God so that, by
exercising their proper function and being led by the
spirit of the gospel, they can work for the
sanctification of the world from within, in the
manner of leaven. In this way they can make Christ
known to others, especially by the testimony of a life
resplendent in faith, hope, and charity. The layman
is closely involved in temporal affairs of every sort.
It is therefore his special task to illumine and
organize these affairs in such a way that they may
always start out, develop and persist according to
Christ's mind, to the praise of the Creator and
Redeemer. (*Dogmatic Constitution on the Church*, #31)

Catechism of the Catholic Church. How are we to respond
to God's call?

Those who with God's help have welcomed Christ's
call and freely responded to it are urged on by love
of Christ to proclaim the Good News everywhere in
the world. This treasure, received from the apostles,

has been faithfully guarded by their successors. All Christ's faithful are called to hand it on from generation to generation, by professing the faith, by living it in fraternal sharing, and by celebrating it in liturgy and prayer (Cf. Acts 2:42). (#3)

Contemporary Reading. *Are we all called to be pilgrims and exiles? Why?*

I believe my vocation is essentially that of a pilgrim and an exile in life, that I have no proper place in this world but that for that reason I am in some sense to be the friend and brother of people everywhere, especially those who are exiles and pilgrims like myself.... My life is in many ways simple, but it is also a mystery which I do not attempt to really understand, as though I were led by the hand in a night where I see nothing, but can fully depend on the Love and Protection of Him who guides me.[3]

Notes

[1] Nine-year-old Mary in *The Spiritual Life of Children*, by Robert Coles (Boston: Houghton Mifflin Company, 1990), pp. 135-136.

[2] See *Dogmatic Constitution on the Church*, #39.

[3] *The Hidden Ground of Love: The Letters of Thomas Merton on Religious Experience and Social Concerns*, selected and edited by William H. Shannon (New York: Farrar Straus Giroux, 1985), p. 52.

DAY FOUR
Loving a Redeeming God

Coming Together in the Spirit

In the movie *Ordinary People* there is a scene in which the tension at a Thanksgiving dinner ends with the breaking of a platter. The mother picks it up, holds the two large pieces together and exclaims that there is nothing wrong. Facts belie the statement.

Defining Our Thematic Context

There *is* something wrong—not only with our platters but, tragically, with our relationships. Denial doesn't get us off the hook. One dimension of our spiritual journey calls us to review the totality of our relationship with God. We have prayed over the mystery of existence, the powerful providence of God, our vocation to participate in God's creative design. We come now before the awesome mystery of sin, our individual sinfulness as well as our collective guilt.

A month before she died, Jessica Powers participated in a long session of selecting poems for publication. Sister Regina Siegfried and I sat with her as we carefully read through poem after poem. After our work had been completed, the question came up as to the ordering of the poems. Jessica had no argument against putting the poems into various categories rather than presenting them chronologically. But she was firm about what should be the first and last poems in the edition.

The last would be "Doxology," a poem in praise of the triune God. No surprise here: This fit in well with the entire Carmelite liturgical life, with the prayer of the Church. But what would be the first poem, which was to set a tone for the entire volume?

Jessica Powers was a realist, no romantic. She knew the need for redemption, she knew the mystery of sin and the cost that personal and collective sin imposed on history. Her first poem would be about the mercy of God, a mercy that won for us redemption. To be on retreat with Jessica Powers is to plunge deeply into the mystery of sin and to taste the wine of God's tender mercy.

What is essential here is focus. The danger is to become fixated on ourselves and thereby forget about the power and centrality of divine forgiveness. The danger is to get caught in the web of one's own shame and humiliation. Jessica would have us clutch the garments of God and never turn our gaze away from God's mercy. She invites us to join her: "I walked out of myself and went into the woods of God's mercy."[1] Walk with her in that most important journey.

Opening Prayer

> Be with us, Lord,
>   as we venture into the darkness called sin.
> We have sinned
>   and have not lived as your sons and daughters.
> Turn your eyes of mercy toward us.
> Draw us to the foot of the cross

that we may see, full-face,
the evil we have done—
but even more, your redemptive love and mercy.
Heal our broken relationships
and restore us to your gentle peace.
We make this prayer through Jesus,
our savior and redeemer,
our Lord and our life.

RETREAT SESSION FOUR

The Passion of a Redeeming God

A fourth gerund: redeeming. Though God created the world and humankind good, something went wrong. That something we call sin, that choice against love, that breaking of relationships, that disobedience to God's command. We stand in need of salvation. Our redemption comes through the cross and the forgiveness of sin. Herein is our freedom, our hope, our peace.

Jessica Powers' theme song is the mercy of God. God's love in the face of sin is mercy. God's love redeems us and restores us to righteousness. For Jessica Powers, an image of this redeeming God is a divine repairer of fences.

Repairer of Fences

I am alone in the dark, and I am thinking
what darkness would be mine if I could see
the ruin I wrought in every place I wandered
and if I could not be

aware of One who follows after me.
Whom do I love, O God, when I love Thee?
The great Undoer who has torn apart
the walls I built against a human heart,
the Mender who has sewn together the hedges
through which I broke when I went seeking ill,
the Love who follows and forgives me still.
Fumbler and fool that I am, with things around me
of fragile make like souls, how I am blessed
to hear behind me footsteps of a Savior!
I sing to the east; I sing to the west:
God is my repairer of fences, turning my paths
    into rest.

Isaiah 58:12 (Douay)

For Reflection

- *Take five small fragments of paper and write on them five sins you want to bring to the Lord.*

- *In your heart whisper slowly "Kyrie eleison" ("Lord, have mercy").*

- *Take a cross and gaze intently at it, the symbol of God's redemptive love.*

Admitting our sinfulness is dangerous turf, easily becoming quicksand. Our focus can center on self and the abuse of freedom, drawing us to discouragement, perhaps even despair. Our gaze must be twofold: facing the mirror of sin but always in the light of God's mercy. Without moving too quickly to the assurance of forgiveness, we do know that grace abounds over sin.

There *is* something wrong. The list is substantial: disobedience to God's commandments, choices against love, the broken web of relationships, the violence of hatred and racism, the neglect of duty, the moods of indifference, crass greed, destructive consumerism. Daily newspapers provide the details.

And how does God deal with sin? The cross reveals the extravagance of God's mercy as surely as it shows the horror of sin. Mercy is God's love in the face of sin. Our hope lies not in repentant mortification, important as that is. Rather, we put our confidence in the Lord, who forgives seventy times seven times.

Our rich Christian tradition is filled with references to the mystery of an indwelling God. True, God is transcendent, totally other; yet God is also immanent, totally near. As a poet, Jessica Powers often wrote about this mystery. In her poem "The Place of Splendor," she cries out: "Child, have none told you? *God* is in your soul." And the God who dwelt in Jessica Powers' soul wore special garments, the robes of divine mercy. Listen intently and prayerfully to this song of full-strength faith.

The Garments of God

God sits on a chair of darkness in my soul.
He is God alone, supreme in His majesty.
I sit at His feet, a child in the dark beside Him;
my joy is aware of His glance and my sorrow is tempted
to nest on the thought that His face is turned from me.
He is clothed in the robes of His mercy, voluminous garments—
not velvet or silk and affable to the touch,
but fabric strong for a frantic hand to clutch,

and I hold to it fast with the fingers of my will.
Here is my cry of faith, my deep avowal
to the Divinity that I am dust.
Here is the loud profession of my trust.
I need not go abroad
to the hills of speech or the hinterlands of music
for a crier to walk in my soul where all is still.
I have this potent prayer through good or ill:
here in the dark I clutch the garments of God.

Temptations are of various kinds: minor and major, recent and old, playful and deadly. A deadly temptation is to think that God's eyes have forever been turned away from us. One of the effects of sin is to see ourselves as now rejected by God, as having placed ourselves beyond the reach of God's love, beyond the gaze of divine forgiveness. The temptation slides us further and further into isolation and a sense of abandonment. Faith tells us that God cannot not love; that God's gaze is always upon us; that our attributions to God of severe anger and wrath arise out of sinful projection. Jesus came not for the healthy but for the sick. Jesus searches out the lost and the least.

God's garments of mercy are made of sturdy stuff. How else can we grab hold and hang on with "the fingers of our will"? No romanticism here, no soft cooing and wooing. Jessica Powers confronts facts that cause no small dread and fright. Awareness of the infinite distance between God's extravagant goodness and our turning away from the light causes deep anxiety. Were not the garments we clutch voluminous and strong, all would be lost.

So we make our cry of faith and take ownership of our identity as sinners. But that cry is at the very same time a proclamation of hope and trust. It's a silent cry that does not invoke dirges and dramatic wailing. Sin reduces us to silent shame and profound humility. Indeed, though our guilt is always before us, the light of God's merciful gaze continues to burn brightly.

Is clutching a good form of prayer? Sometimes it is the only form available to us. It may well express the deepest level of faith since there is so little of self involved. As a frightened child clings to its mother, so we are invited to cling to the garments of God's mercy.

And all of this in the dark, the darkness of deep faith. We do not see the eyes of God. We do not have certitude of being cleansed. We sit and kneel and hope in the dark that God's redemptive love is transforming our very being. If peace and joy arise, how blest is that soul. If no feelings arise, our faith will hopefully sustain us. In the end, we hold tightly to garments that are suddenly transformed into a wedding robe.

For Reflection

- *What type of chair does God sit on in your soul?*

- *What do you do when the temptation to "nest on the thought that his face is turned from me" comes?*

- *What is your most potent prayer?*

Closing Prayer

Slowly reread the poem "The Garments of God" (see page 55). Sit at the feet of God with Jessica Powers and clutch the divine garments. Share together the wonderful story of Jesus' forgiveness of the woman caught in adultery (below). Let that woman share with you her experience of God's love. Together ponder the mission of Jesus—not only to the woman about to be stoned, but to the entire world. How is obedience inseparable from redemption? Note that those clutching the garments of God are all sinners and that all are welcome. Do you sit at table with sinners? How does self-forgiveness fit into all of this? Do you think the woman Jesus forgave was able to forgive herself? Reflect on these readings with Jessica.

God's Word. *Where do you find yourself in this story?*

> Early in the morning [Jesus] came again to the temple. All the people came to him and he sat down and began to teach them. The scribes and the Pharisees brought a woman who had been caught in adultery; and making her stand before all of them, they said to him, "Teacher, this woman was caught in the very act of committing adultery. Now in the law, Moses commanded us to stone such women. Now what do you say?" They said this to test him, so that they might have some charge to bring against him. Jesus bent down and wrote with his finger on the ground. When they kept on questioning him, he straightened up and said to them, "Let anyone among you who is without sin be the first to throw a stone at her." And once again he bent down and wrote on the ground. When they heard it, they went away, one by one, beginning with the elders; and Jesus was left alone with the woman standing before him. Jesus straightened up and said to her, "Woman, where are they? Has no one condemned you?" She said, "No one, sir." And Jesus said, "Neither do I condemn you. Go your way, and from now on do not sin again." (John 8:2-11)

Second Vatican Council. *How is our redemption achieved?*

The Son, therefore, came on mission from His Father. It was in Him, before the foundation of the world, that the Father chose us and predestined us to become adopted sons, for in Him it has pleased the Father to reestablish all things. To carry out the will of the Father, Christ inaugurated the kingdom of heaven on earth and revealed to us the mystery of the Father. By His obedience He brought about redemption. The Church, or, in other words, the kingdom of Christ now present in mystery, grows visibly in the world through the power of God. (*Dogmatic Constitution on the Church,* #3)

Catechism of the Catholic Church. What is the quality of your mercy?

Jesus gave scandal above all when he identified his merciful conduct toward sinners with God's own attitude toward them (cf. Matthew 9:13; Hosea 6:6). He went so far as to hint that by sharing the table of sinners he was admitting them to the messianic banquet (cf. Luke 15:1-2, 22-32). But it was most especially by forgiving sins that Jesus placed the religious authorities of Israel on the horns of a dilemma. Were they not entitled to demand in consternation, "Who can forgive sins but God alone?" (Mark 2:7). By forgiving sins Jesus either is blaspheming as a man who made himself God's equal or is speaking the truth, and his person really does make present and reveal God's name (cf. John 5:18; 10:33; 17:6, 26). (#589)

Contemporary Writing. *What is the important thing to learn about sin?*

He has no religion, but I could not write to him in other than religious terms, because what I had to write to him about was nothing less than the forgiveness of sins. How can one write about that except in those terms? Who forgives sins except God and the person I sin against? There is only one other person who can forgive me, and that is I myself. But to forgive myself when I know no God, and when I am separated from those I sinned against by prison walls and thousands of miles of ocean, is surely impossible. Therefore I took it upon myself to say that those whom Lester had sinned against had now forgiven him, and that I did not know of any one of us who had not forgiven him. Therefore he must forgive himself. The important thing to learn about sin is not that nothing can reduce the sinfulness of past sins. What is important is that they can be forgiven, and that, once they are forgiven, one must at all costs forgive oneself.[2]

Notes

[1] "The Mercy of God."

[2] Alan Paton, *For You Departed* (New York: Charles Scribner's Sons, 1969), p. 150.

DAY FIVE
Loving a Challenging God

Coming Together in the Spirit

Our creating and sustaining God also calls us to ministry and redeems us of sin. God then challenges us to grow, to be fully alive in grace. In other words, God is demanding. Would that we had the journal of the man who ran up to Jesus, knelt before him, and inquired what he must do to inherit eternal life (see Mark 10:17-22). It might read something like this:

> Today I met Jesus. When I asked what I must do to inherit everlasting life, he inquired of me if I had kept all the commandments. I said yes. Then Jesus looked at me with love and indicated that I lack one thing: poverty! What demands he makes in following him: Sell everything and give all my money to the poor. I was shocked and went away sad.

Defining Our Thematic Context

Those who love us desire our growth and are willing to challenge us to be the best we can be. God is a challenger, longing for us to live life to the full. John's Gospel is clear: "I came that they may have life, and have it abundantly" (John 10:10b). Implicit in that challenge is the need for discipline and a dying to one's old self. Serious stuff here: painful transformation leading to blessed communion. Daily the Lord invites us down to the potter's house to shape and mold our lives into holiness (see Jeremiah 18:1-11).

Discipleship involves the cross. Those who wish to follow Jesus, to live a Godward life, must be willing to bear hardship, to embrace persecution, to accept death. It is not surprising that many walk away—it's just too demanding a journey. But grace is offered. Gifted with the power of the Spirit and supported, I hope, by a caring community, we can bear the cross and even find within it the grace of joy.

On Day Five of our retreat we will have the opportunity to examine God's gentle but firm prodding. If the heart is to be abundant, if the Kingdom is to be realized, we must be forced beyond our narrow limits into abundant life.

In a poem evoking the gift of the Spirit, Jessica Powers shows us God challenging us to achieve summer's full growth:

Come South Wind

"By south wind is meant the Holy Spirit who awakens love."
Saint John of the Cross

Over and over I say to the south wind: come,
waken in me and warm me!
I have walked too long with a death's chill in the air,
mourned over trees too long with branches bare.
Ice has a falsity for all its brightness
and so has need of your warm reprimand.
A curse be on the snow that lapsed from whiteness,

and all bleak days that paralyze my land.

I am saying all day to Love who wakens love:
rise in the south and come!
Hurry me into springtime; hustle the winter
out of my sight; make dumb
the north wind's loud impertinence. Then plunge me
into my leafing and my blossoming,
and give me pasture, sweet and sudden pasture.
Where could the Shepherd bring
his flocks to graze? Where could they rest at
noonday?
O south wind, listen to the woe I sing!
One whom I love is asking for the summer
from me, who still am distances from spring.

Opening Prayer

God of truth and glory,
   your plan of salvation embraced suffering and
death.
You are a strange Lover,
   refusing to spoil us with soft wiles
   or woo us with balmy words.

Your love is strong, stronger than death;
   your concern is deep, deeper than the sea;
   your compassion is noble, nobler than the stars of
      night.

Send your Spirit into our hearts
   that we may accept your challenge to fullness of life
   and bear our crosses with dignity and courage.

Help us to interpret aright your demands.

Bless us with wisdom to know what is pleasing to you
   and to accept the limitations that life imposes.
Then, with Jesus, your Son,
   we will radiate the glory found in those
   who endure all things
   with joy and thanksgiving. Amen.

For Reflection

- *Take a crucifix and gaze intently at it for five minutes.*

- *Jot down three human demands and three divine demands from your own history.*

- *Who were your best teachers? What did they demand of you?*

RETREAT SESSION FIVE

The Passion of a Challenging God

Relationships are dynamic, constantly in flux. If they are not being nourished or challenged, they tend toward diminishment, even regression. This is true in our families and friendships; this is true in our relationship with God.

Our spiritual director, Jessica Powers, knew the many faces of God: Christ the Lover, his radiant face wet with tears (see "The Mountains of the Lord"); the God who "smiles on faith that seems to know / it has no other place to go" ("Prayer"); a God who "likes to see me lifting to His eyes / even the wretchedness that dropped His grace" ("Creature of God"). Behind the poetry of Jessica Powers one can feel the writings of John of the Cross and, in particular, the theme that "when God looks, he loves." Delight is love's flower. Rejoicing in the beloved, during all seasons, speaks of the fidelity of a passionate God.

In a 1987 Ash Wednesday letter, Jessica Powers wrote to me:

> There are graces in the writings of those not of our faith, aren't there? Sometimes lovely things that are lost. Beautiful things God scatters everywhere. As Walt Whitman said (in other words), that God is tossing down love letters in the streets and everywhere, if only we would watch out for them. I think I have come to see that even the contradictions and crosses of life are His "love letters." I've begun to look for them with a certain joy—signs that tell me that Jesus is near. The unexpected delay, the negative response, the inopportune caller, the gimmick that won't work, the nice food that got overcooked, the lack of something needed, the ballpoint pen that smudges, the mistake one can't undo—the list is endless![1]

Thus the poet shares her experience of a challenging God who invites us to see life from the perspective of faith—and to grasp the possibility that our God is a strange Lover. God does not allow us to get our own way when it means destroying ourselves and probably others. But the love letters come, one after the other in myriad circumstances. Jessica Powers invites us to see life from a different point of view, to see that God is concerned for our ultimate well-being.

Retreat is a time to reexamine our notion of God and the very meaning of life. Jessica Powers loves a God who is demanding, challenging, unrelenting in his desire for union with us. Whatever would intervene must be scrutinized, often rejected. It is not surprising that many walk away from the God revealed in Jesus, a God who calls us to sacrifice our nearest and dearest if they become obstacles on the way to salvation. Ask for the grace of courage as you venture into these deep waters.

Jessica Powers knew the demands of God. The rigorous penances of cloistered life, the pains of physical suffering, the dark night of the soul—crosses and sufferings which, when transformed, lead to growth. Out of love God challenges us to be fully alive and invites us to share the glory of the resurrection.

In describing the mystery of grace, Saint Augustine wrote: "Because you have loved me, O Lord, you have made me lovable." God is love, so says Saint John (1 John 4:8b). But divine love is trillions of light years from our human, romantic concepts of love. God's love endures all things, bears all things, believes all things (see 1 Corinthians 13:7).

Not surprisingly, we find God to be a strange Lover. Jessica Powers found this also. Listen to her words and ponder them carefully:

God Is a Strange Lover

God is the strangest of all lovers; His ways are past
  explaining.
He sets His heart on a soul; He says to Himself, "Here
  will

  I rest My love."
But He does not woo her with flowers or jewels or
  words that

  are set to music,

no names endearing, no kindled praise His heart's
  direction
                              prove.
His jealousy is an infinite thing. He stalks the soul
                      with sorrows;
He tramples the bloom; He blots the sun that could
  make
                      her vision dim.
He robs and breaks and destroys—there is nothing at
  last but
                      her own shame, her own affliction,
and then He comes and there is nothing in the vast
  world but
                      Him and her love of Him.

Not till the great rebellions die and her will is safe in
  His
                      hands forever
does He open the door of light and His tendernesses
  fall,
and then for what is seen in the soul's virgin places,
for what is heard in the heart, there is no speech at all.

God is a strange lover; the story of His love is most
  surprising.
There is no proud queen in her cloth of gold; over and
  over again
there is only, deep in the soul, a poor disheveled
  woman weeping...
for us who have need of a picture and words: the
  Magdalen.

What would you think of a deity that "stalks the soul
with sorrows" or "robs and beats and destroys" or lets
the beloved know only shame and sorrow? A strange
deity, that! Would you call that God a lover?

Yet certain souls have experienced God as the strangest of all lovers. Jessica Powers was one; John Donne, another. Listen to Donne's sonnet where he even asks God to be demanding in order that union may be experienced by the poet:

Batter my heart, three-personed God, for you
   As yet but knock, breathe, shine, and seek to mend;
   That I may rise and stand, o'erthrow me and bend
Your force to break, blow, burn, and make me new.
I, like an usurped town to another due,
   Labour to admit you, but O, to no end.
Reason, your viceroy in me, me should defend,
But is captived and proves weak or untrue.
Yet dearly I love you and would be loved fain,
   But am betrothed unto your enemy.

Divorce me, untie, or break that knot again,
   Take me to you, imprison me, for I,
      Except you enthrall me, never shall be free,
      Nor ever chaste except you ravish me.[2]

Is all this poetry a manifestation of spiritual pathology, to be abhorred and condemned as the work of a fanatic? Or is this verse an expression of ultimate longing for intimacy and union that refuses to let anything get in the way, such as flowers or jewels or musical words? Love does strange things to achieve its goal of oneness. As Dostoevsky says in *The Brothers Karamazov*: "Love in action is a harsh and dreadful thing compared to love in dreams."

The story of God's love is a story of challenge. Abraham's faith was tested at Mount Moriah; Mary's faith was tested by the message of an angel; Peter's faith was tested on a hill called Calvary. God wants the whole of our minds and hearts and souls. The words of the Our Father—"lead us not into temptation"—take on a new meaning when we hear the sound of the Hound's feet in fast pursuit.

In each of our lives there are small and great rebellions, our will seeking self-interest, come what may. Then the need for harsh discipline; then the need for mortification that leads to life and freedom. Once our will is under the banner of God's standard, then the tendernesses can and do fall. No words or gifts are necessary once lovers are together. Now love can rest, now peace come.

In another poem, "Not Garden Any More," Jessica Powers writes: "God is not garden anymore, to satiate the senses with the luxuriance of full exotic wilderness." Rather, God has become a desert filled with divine tremendous loneliness. God lures the soul "that I might hear in silence / this infinite outcry of His solitude." The reason God is a strange Lover is because God is simply strange, unfamiliar to our human system of judging and evaluating. Our God rejects all idolatry and goes for the heart. All else is expendable. God reverses and turns upside down our perceptions of what is real. A strange, tender, loving, passionate Lover is our God.

For Reflection

- *What are your images of God? Where do they come from?*

- *Are you comfortable with a demanding God who asks for everything? Why?*

- *What are God's demands and challenges today?*

- *What is God currently asking of you?*

Closing Prayer

Sit with Jessica Powers in the presence of the Lord. Together ponder the question of love. How do you "prove" your love of God? How do you demonstrate your genuine response to the call to discipleship? How does Jesus call to you in your conscience? What demands do you hear and follow? Which have you denied and abandoned? Is the God of Moses and Abraham demanding? Does God demand from us what God demanded from them? Is life a comedy or a tragedy? In the end what can we expect? Let Jessica offer you her reflections on these questions—and your response.

God's Word. *Why is the deepest challenge always that of love?*

> When they had finished breakfast, Jesus said to Simon Peter, "Simon son of John, do you love me more than these?" He said to him, "Yes, Lord; you know that I love you." Jesus said to him, "Feed my lambs." A second time he said to him, "Simon son of John, do you love me?" He said to him, "Yes, Lord, you know that I love you." Jesus said to him, "Tend my sheep." He said to him the third time, "Simon son of John, do you love me?" Peter felt hurt because he said to him the third time, "Do you love me?" And he said to him: "Lord, you know everything; you know that I love you." Jesus said to him, "Feed my sheep." (John 21:15-17)

Second Vatican Council. *Why does God demand obedience from us?*

> In the depth of his conscience, man detects a law which he does not impose upon himself, but which

holds him to obedience. Always summoning him to love good and avoid evil, the voice of conscience can when necessary speak to his heart more specifically: Do this, shun that. For man has in his heart a law written by God. To obey it is the very dignity of man; according to it he will be judged. (*Pastoral Constitution on the Church in the Modern World*, #16)

Catechism of the Catholic Church. In what way is God a strange God?

God calls Moses from the midst of a bush that burns without being consumed: "I am the God of your father, the God of Abraham, the God of Isaac, and the God of Jacob" (Exodus 3:6). God is the God of the fathers, the One who had called and guided the patriarchs in their wanderings. He is the faithful and compassionate God who remembers them and his promises; he comes to free their descendants from slavery. He is the God who, from beyond space and time, can do this and wills to do it, the God who will put his almighty power to work for this plan. (#205)

Contemporary Writing. *Why is choosing to live with God so dangerous?*

Wiesel put aside his prepared script and spoke directly to Rubenstein's concern, pointing out that if it is hard to live a life of negation, it is even harder to live a life of affirmation. "If you want difficulties," he said, "choose to live with God. Can you compare the tragedy of the believer to that of the nonbeliever? The real tragedy, the real drama, is the drama of the believer."[3]

Notes

[1] Robert F. Morneau, *Mantras From a Poet: Jessica Powers* (Sheed & Ward, 1991), p. viii.

[2] "Holy Sonnets," *The New Oxford Book of English Verse: 1250-1950,* chosen and edited by Helen Gardner (New York: Oxford University Press, 1972), p. 198.

[3] Robert McAfee Brown, *Creative Dislocation: The Movement of Grace* (Nashville: Abingdon, 1980), p. 91.

DAY SIX
Loving a Delighting God

Coming Together in the Spirit

The priest-poet George Herbert (1593-1633) describes God's longing for intimacy with the soul:

Love

Love bade me welcome; yet my soul drew back,
    Guilty of dust and sin.
But quick-ey'd Love, observing me grow slack
    From my first entrance in,
Drew nearer to me, sweetly questioning,
    If I lack'd anything.

A guest, I answer'd, worthy to be here:
    Love said, You shall be he.
I the unkind, ungrateful? Ah my dear,
    I cannot look on thee.
Love took my hand, and smiling did reply,
    Who made the eyes but I?

Truth Lord, but I have marr'd them: let my shame
    Go where it doth deserve.
And know you not, says Love, who bore the blame?
    My dear, then I will serve.
You must sit down, says Love, and taste my meat:
    So I did sit and eat.

Defining Our Thematic Context

Discipleship, the following of Jesus, is a costly affair. The cross indicates that. But there is another dimension in the life of the disciple that provides the basis for carrying the cross. That dimension is friendship.

In John's Gospel Jesus instructs his followers: No longer are they mere servants, fulfilling the numerous duties and demands of servanthood. Rather, they are friends, friends of God. And this gift of friendship is freely given: Jesus has chosen them, not vice-versa (see John 15:12-17).

Amazing grace, indeed. Our creating, sustaining, redeeming and challenging God is also a God who passionately delights in his creatures. If we need an image for this we turn to the table, that place where life and bread is broken and shared. Friendship is eucharistic because it is filled with love and thanksgiving.

Opening Prayer

God of infinite joy,
>   your love exceeds our wildest expectations,
>   your fondness for us baffles our small-minded
>   faith.
Grant us the grace to experience your smile;
>   still all our fears of your frown.
Your prophet Isaiah tells us
>   that we are precious in your sight;
>   may we take this truth deep into our hearts.
Your apostle Paul tells us
>   nothing can separate us from your love;
>   may we always live in union with you.
Give us again the joy of our youth

as we recognize and acknowledge your abiding
  presence.
Drive all anxiety from our hearts
  and indwell again at our table.
Tasting your delight,
  nourished by your love,
    we will go forth to share the Good News. Amen.

For Reflection

- *Sit at a table, light a candle and read chapter 15 of Saint John's Gospel.*

- *Find a portrait of a smiling Jesus and imprint it in your imagination.*

- *List five reasons why the Lord delights in you.*

RETREAT SESSION SIX

The Passion of a Delighting God

The psalms tell us that God delights in the children of creation. A God who delights, a God who rejoices in his family and enjoys being with them.

The psalmist tells us that God delights in the children of the universe. A God who delights! This is a far cry from the images of God communicated by an unbalanced reading of Scripture that shows God as harsh, condemning. What a contrast to images of God which would have us living in continual fear and trepidation! The symbol for delight is a smile, a facial expression of acceptance and warmth and love. This is news some may find too good to be true. One who delights in us, takes pleasure in us, enjoys our company—such is our God. This is not to negate judgment and accountability. But we have a God who knows dance and song and festivity.

The mystery of God is so vast, our language systems so limited. Poet Jessica Powers turns to metaphor to describe God's Spirit, a Spirit who breathes upon creation. If we listen intensely we can feel the intimacy of God, the delight of God, the God of surprises:

The Spirit's Name

Dove is the name of Him and so is Flame,
and love can push aside all eager symbols
to be His peerless and His proper name.
And Wind and Water, even Cloud will do,
if it is heart that has the interview.

But when at last you are alone with Him
deep in the soul and past the senses' choir,
Oh, give Him then that title which will place
His unpredictable breath upon your face:
O Dove, O Flame, O Water, Wind and Cloud!
(And here the creature wings go veering higher)
O love that lifts us wholly into God!

O Deifier.

Jessica Powers wrote to me on July 15, 1985: "Enclosed are two poems which you may like. The one by e. e. cummings is a recent finding 'i am a little church (no great cathedral)'. Isn't it lovely? 'to / merciful Him Whose only now is forever.'[1] And the one by Mark Van Doren reminds me of what our father St. John of the Cross said of the glance of God: how when God looks at a

76

soul He makes it beautiful."

Jessica Powers' God is a God who loves his creatures and takes delight in them. Following the thought from the First Letter of John that "God is love,"[2] she rejoices in the words of John of the Cross, who claims that God's very look must always be one of love. Of course, in the presence of sin that divine look is interpreted by some as anger.

Beneath the poetry of Jessica Powers one can feel a God of profound joy. The paradox here is that joy does not exclude suffering and pain. The essence of the spiritual journey for Jessica Powers is presence: the presence of a creating God, the presence of a Savior, the presence of the Spirit.

Jessica Powers incarnated the divine characteristic of delight on her journey. She relished her community and friends, taking great delight in their presence. Often she would tell tales at supper, causing abundant laughter. Wit was one of her gifts and she shared it well, bringing to others a part of her baptismal mission. And, of course, her poetry brought extravagant joy—and still does—to those who ponder its inner recesses.

Inebriation breaks down our ego boundaries, lifting us out of ourselves into a certain spacelessness. When the agent is alcohol or drugs, the adventure can turn dangerous and destructive. But there is also a holy inebriation: ecstasy. Love breaks down our egotism and lifts us to the plane of intimacy and union. It is possible to be drunk, but not with wine. Quietly, joyfully reflect on Jessica Power's commentary on the prophet Isaiah:

But Not With Wine

"You are drunk, but not with wine." Isaiah 51:21.

O God of too much giving, whence is this

inebriation that possesses me,
that the staid road now wanders all amiss
and that the wind walks much too giddily,
clutching a bush for balance, or a tree?
How then can dignity and pride endure
with such inordinate mirth upon the land,
when steps and speech are somewhat insecure
and the light heart is wholly out of hand?

If there be indecorum in my songs,
fasten the blame where rightly it belongs:
on Him who offered me too many cups
of His most potent goodness—not on me,
a peasant who, because a king was host,
drank out of courtesy.

For Reflection

- *Have you ever been overwhelmed by too many gifts?*

- *How have you experienced God's most potent goodness?*

- *Is drinking out of courtesy good or bad? Does it remove responsibility?*

- *Can mirth be inordinate? When has it been for you?*

- *When are you lighthearted? What are the causes?*

Philosophers tell us that moderation (temperance) is a moral virtue that protects us from extremes. Too much food, drink, power, pleasure turns destructive; too little can inhibit growth and block the legitimate pleasures of life. The advice is to fulfill appropriate needs while exercising discipline in the field of wants.

Poets are less cautious; they experience exuberance in the mystery called life. Exaltation and despair, inebriation and radical asceticism, infatuating hopes and crippling despair are the experiences that stimulate the deepest writings.

Jessica Powers knew deep suffering; she also knew deep joy. The source of delight arises out of the goodness of God, who invites women and men to the divine banquet. Cana is a symbol of God's desire to celebrate love and life—gallons upon gallons of new wine to be drunk "out of courtesy."

Prohibitionists are here scandalized. Even to hint that God might be a remote cause for inebriation is blasphemous. Yet it is in the offer of friendship that the soul is lifted out of its egotistical corral to rejoice in the spaciousness of God's garden. No longer are we to sing quietly. No longer is indecorum a sign of rude manners. Now the soul is liberated from confining roles that stifle and dampen the spirit. Our singing lifts us to new intimacies and draws us into deeper commitments.

When self-righteous or even thoughtful leaders point a finger of accusation our way, we need not assume the whole responsibility. The drink offered in such quantity was not sought. It is sheer gift, sheer grace. And not to drink of such friendship would be the real sin. Yet those who have never had their elbows on the holy table will never know what they have missed or what new promises are given.

Closing Prayer

Sit with Jessica Powers and reflect reverently on the mystery of the friendship that God offers us. Experience the power of divine life given us through Baptism and our sacramental life. Note how God gives us family and community to manifest his love and delight. Do you take these blessings for granted? Further, are you able to find in our dependence upon God the joy and delight hidden in our creaturehood? How do you express your praise and gratitude for a God who delights in you?

God's Word. *How do we become friends of God?*

> This is my commandment, that you love one another as I have loved you. No one has greater love than this, to lay down one's life for one's friends. You are my friends if you do what I command you. I do not call you servants any longer, because the servant does not know what the master is doing; but I have called you friends, because I have made known to you everything that I have heard from my Father. (John 15:12-15)

Second Vatican Council. *How does a Christian family reflect the friendship of God?*

> Thus the Christian family, which springs from marriage as a reflection of the loving covenant uniting Christ with the Church, and as a participation in that covenant, will manifest to all men the Savior's living presence in the world, and the genuine nature of the Church. This the family will do by the mutual love of the spouses, by their generous fruitfulness, their solidarity and faithfulness, and by the loving way in which all members of the family work together. (*Pastoral*

Catechism of the Catholic Church. *What is the source of Christian joy?*

> With creation, God does not abandon his creatures to themselves. He not only gives them being and existence, but also, and at every moment, upholds and sustains them in being, enables them to act and brings them to their final end. Recognizing this utter dependence with respect to the Creator is a source of wisdom and freedom, of joy and confidence. (#301)

Contemporary Writing. *How familiar are you with God?*

> "Oh, Lord," he prayed, "I put myself in Your hands. Without you I am no better than a crow, going nowhere. Without you I am alone, no more than smoke rising through the chimney and disappearing in the air. You know my situation. I put myself in Your hands, Father. Amen."
>
> His body relaxed and he sat up straighter. He liked talking to God better than anything in the world. Before he went to sleep at night, he knelt beside the bed and prayed, and sometimes awoke the next morning to find that he'd fallen asleep on his knees. He told God everything—about not burying Poppa on the hillside and feeling guilty for thinking that Poppa didn't deserve to be buried there, about Momma not wanting to live and how she sat in her room rocking back and forth and when he brought her supper she called him Charles and tried to kiss him like she had Poppa. Mostly when Joshua prayed, however, he told God how much he loved Him. Sometimes he just quoted verses from psalms he'd memorized.[3]

Notes

[1] e.e. cummings, *Complete Poems: 1904-1962* (New York: Liveright Publishing Corporation, 1958, 1986, 1991).

[2] See 1 John 4:8b.

[3] Julius Lester, *Do Lord Remember Me* (New York: Holt, Rinehart and Winston, 1984), p. 46.

DAY SEVEN
Loving a Commissioning God

Coming Together in the Spirit

Jessica Powers told me in a letter dated Palm Sunday, 1987: "My poetry department is in disorder; I haven't found time to straighten it out, nor the ambition right now. My only purpose in writing is that there are things I would like to say to everyone, especially those who are turning away from God. But I do not know if they would find grace in any words of mine."

Defining Our Thematic Context

Love eventually demands action. God is love. Thus, the Creator, Sustainer and Redeemer also becomes the divine Commissioner. Love cannot sit and stare; love is active and giving to the point of total self-donation. The paschal mystery, the life and death and resurrection of Jesus, informs our Christian theology. Jesus was sent on a mission and his ministry is our own.

A sending forth (mission) is at the heart of every religion, so much so that evangelization is defined as one of the main purposes of religious behavior. Jessica Powers knew herself called and sent. Her poetry acknowledges her commissioning.

Opening Prayer

Lord God, as you sent forth your Spirit,
so too you send us forth
as agents of your kingdom.
Clarify your call to us,
give us courage to do whatever is asked.
May we come to realize the dignity of our unique
vocation
and rejoice in its entrustment.
Show us the heart of Mary
as we attempt to emulate her commitment.
Send us forth with joy and trust. Amen.

For Reflection

- *Make a list of times you were "sent" on a special mission to do or to get something.*

- *Read Jeremiah 1:4-10. Note the elements in this commissioning story.*

- *In the next few days commission someone to do (or make) something for you.*

RETREAT SESSION SEVEN

The Passion of a Commissioning God

Saint Paul tells us that, because of our life in Christ, we are God's ambassadors, agents of reconciliation (see 2 Corinthians 5:20). Jessica Powers saw herself as an ambassador of God, a citizen of love, a member of a little nation whose effective weapon is love. She was commissioned to be a listener and a lover.

The Little Nation

Having no gift of strategy or arms,
no secret weapon and no walled defense,
I shall become a citizen of love,
that little nation with the blood-stained sod
where even the slain have power, the only country
that sends forth an ambassador to God.

Renouncing self and crying out to evil
to end its wars, I seek a land that lies
all unprotected like a sleeping child;
nor is my journey reckless and unwise.
Who doubts that love has an effective weapon
may meet with a surprise.

Jessica Powers was a Carmelite religious. Hers was a life of prayer and penance, of community and worship. Within that "commissioning" by God she was also given another task: writing. Her motive was ultimately to lead people to God, to pray that her words might be instruments of grace. Like many followers of Christ, she was not given any assurance as to whether or not her mission was effective.

God prodded her in a variety of ways. An eighth-grade teacher affirmed her writings; a poetry society in New York became a source of growth and enrichment; friends across the years wrote to express gratitude for a line or a whole poem. God doesn't give a mission without also giving strength and encouragement.

Yet Jessica Powers had to face that human struggle, that doubt as to the validity of her calling. She had no assurance that sinners would turn to God through her writings. She wrote and hoped. She was faithful to this calling despite the darkness. Our retreat director would consider herself not a guide but a fellow pilgrim. Her words are not answers to questions but simply reflections—often profound—on the action of grace. Her dream was that the grace she had received might be extended to others. Her gift was for the growth of the Body of Christ. Her solitary, contemplative life was essentially missionary in nature.

People who live on a plantation find the concept of pilgrimage disturbing. People who have constructed comfort zones will find the invitation and demands of the gospel irritating. The rich young man of Mark 10:17-22 may well live near the center of our hearts.

Have we a model for the journey? Who else but Mary, the mother of Jesus! Her commission was to bear Jesus and carry him to others. We are baptized into that same mission.

Jessica Powers often wrote about Mary, the mother of Jesus. But the poet refused to sentimentalize the unique vocation given to Mary, who knew the sword that pierced the heart and felt the weight of the cross' cruelty. Realism and honesty surround the commissioning done by God. Salvation is a costly adventure. Just as Jesus was sent into the crucible of suffering and death in order to rise, so too Mary and all disciples must drink the cup to the dregs. The miracle is that death leads to life, truth to freedom, love to joy.

Prayerfully join Mary in her commissioning:

The Visitation Journey

The second bead: scene of the lovely journey
of Lady Mary, on whom artists confer

a blue silk gown, a day pouring out Springtime,
and birds singing and flowers bowing to her.

Rather, I see a girl upon a donkey
and her too held by what was said to mind
how the sky was or if the grass was growing.
I doubt the flowers; I doubt the road was kind.

"Love hurried forth to serve." I read, approving.
But also see, with thoughts blown past her youth,
a girl riding upon a jolting donkey
and riding further and further into the truth.

For Reflection

- *What are the first and third beads that surround Mary's visitation?*

- *Why is the description of life as a lovely journey inadequate?*

- *What was the truth into which Mary rode?*

- *Who else rode a donkey because of a unique mission?*

- *Why do some artists have a tendency to romanticize and thus distort reality?*

In Saint Paul's Letter to the Ephesians we are given a game plan. Salvation, freedom from sin, comes through Jesus Christ. Paul knew himself to be commissioned despite his unworthiness. In speech and letters he communicated to the people of his day (and our own) the message of redemption:

Blessed be the God and Father of our Lord Jesus Christ, who has blessed us with every spiritual blessing in the heavenly places, just as he chose us in Christ before the foundation of the world to be holy and blameless before him in love. He destined us for adoption as his children through Jesus Christ, according to the good pleasure of his will, to the praise of his glorious grace that he freely bestowed on us in the Beloved. In him we have redemption through his blood, the forgiveness of our trespasses, according to the riches of his grace that he lavished on us. With all wisdom and insight he has made known to us the mystery of his will, according to his good pleasure that he set forth in Christ, as a plan for the fullness of time, to gather up all things in heaven and things on earth. In Christ we have also obtained an inheritance, having been destined according to the purpose of him who accomplishes all things according to his counsel and will, so that we, who were the first to set our hope on Christ, might live for the praise of his glory. In him you also, when you had heard the word of truth, the gospel of your salvation, and had believed in him, were marked with the seal of the promised Holy Spirit; this is the pledge of our inheritance toward redemption as God's own people, to the praise of his glory. (Ephesians 1:3-14)

No mention is made of two women in this passage, Elizabeth or Mary. Yet, they too were commissioned to play an integral part in the hidden plan of God. Elizabeth would bear a son, John the Baptist, the prophet who prepared the way of the Lord. Mary bore Jesus. Immediately after his conception she carried him to those in need, commissioned to go to whomever was suffering, to whomever was celebrating joy.

How does God commission people? Did Mary receive some inner illumination through the working of the Holy Spirit? Did God utter an audible word such as we hear in daily conversation? Or was Mary's commissioning the work of human need?

As we journey through life the mission given to us will perhaps most frequently arise out of the circumstances of our day. Gandhi responded to the oppression of his country, India, with the mission of liberation. As the AIDS epidemic devastates thousands and thousands of lives, doctors and researchers are commissioned (as professional healers) to combat the disease. Young children in need of an education receive training, skills and knowledge from teachers who believe they have a mission.

But there is something more here than mere human exchange. At times God sends certain individuals to revitalize our way of seeing and acting. We are speaking here of such individuals as Saint Francis of Assisi, Saint Elizabeth Ann Seton, Saint Catherine of Siena, John Henry Cardinal Newman. Each became an instrument of furthering God's kingdom and drawing many people into the circle of light.

Jessica Powers's poem, "The Visitation Journey," carries the implicit reminder that we are never commissioned alone. Jesus dwells within us as he did within Mary. The ultimate result of commissioning is to make Jesus present and manifest. Are we the commissioned ones? We are to "decrease" as, John the Baptist said, the Lord takes his central role in the life of every disciple. Because of this presence, we need not fear. Our trust lies not in our own ability or asceticism. Rather it lies in the Lordship of Jesus.

Jesus made a promise to his disciples: "And remember, I am with you always to the end of the age"

(Matthew 28:20). Mary experienced this promise within her womb. That Presence sustained her mission and her ministry as it does our own. Reflect quietly upon the Advent mystery.

Advent

I live my Advent in the womb of Mary.
And on one night when a great star swings free
from its high mooring and walks down the sky
to be the dot above the *Christus i*,
I shall be born of her by blessed grace.
I wait in Mary-darkness, faith's walled place,
with hope's expectance of nativity.

I knew for long she carried me and fed me,
guarded and loved me, though I could not see.
But only now, with inward jubilee,
I come upon earth's most amazing knowledge:
someone is hidden in this dark with me.

For Reflection

- *What is earth's most amazing knowledge?*

- *Is it possible to live our lives in the womb of God?*

- *What is the source of your hope and expectancy?*

Closing Prayer

Sit with Jessica Powers and discuss Jesus' farewell address and what it means in your life. Dialogue about the missionary nature of the Church, of poetry, of the

Christian life. How do you exercise that activity in your life? Enter into conversation about the ultimate purpose of mission on life's journey. Is this your vision of the Christian life and message? Talk about death. How can death be conceived as the last work of the Christian missionary, of the baptized follower of Jesus?

God's Word. *When has the Lord told you to "go" and make disciples?*

> Now the eleven disciples went to Galilee, to the mountain to which Jesus had directed them. When they saw him, they worshiped him; but some doubted. And Jesus came and said to them, "All authority in heaven and on earth has been given to me. Go therefore and make disciples of all nations, baptizing them in the name of the Father and of the Son and of the Holy Spirit, and teaching them to obey everything that I have commanded you. And remember, I am with you always, to the end of the age." (Matthew 28:16-20)

Second Vatican Council. *What is your sense of mission?*

> It is plain, then, that missionary activity wells up from the Church's innermost nature and spreads abroad her saving faith. It perfects her Catholic unity by expanding it. It is sustained by her apostolicity. It gives expression to the collegial awareness of her hierarchy. It bears witness to her sanctity while spreading and promoting it. (*Decree on the Missionary Activity of the Church*, #6)

Catechism of the Catholic Church. *What is the connection between our call to mission and the mystery of the Trinity?*

The Lord's missionary mandate is ultimately grounded in the eternal love of the Most Holy Trinity: "The Church on earth is by her nature missionary since, according to the plan of the Father, she has as her origin the mission of the Son and the Holy Spirit" (*Decree on the Church's Missionary Activity*, #2). The ultimate purpose of mission is none other than to make men share in the communion between the Father and the Son in their Spirit of love (John Paul II, *Mission of the Redeemer*, #21). (#850)

Contemporary Writing. *How does suffering fit into mission?*

The cross was not something accidental in Jesus' life, but the necessary outcome of his life and of his mission. His death is of decisive significance, not because it alone wrought salvation for us, but because it was the end and fulfillment of his life. In his death he finished the work it was his mission to perform.[1]

Notes

[1] Stanley Hauerwas, *A Community of Character* (Notre Dame, Ind.: University of Notre Dame Press, 1981), p. 48.

Deepening Your Acquaintance

A friend of mine often ended his homily with a provocative question, thereby encouraging the congregation to extend their reflection on the word of God into the week. I can think of no more fitting way to bring this retreat to a conclusion than by extracting from the poetry of Jessica Powers some questions that might allow this retreat to continue far into the future. I list here the ten questions I found most provocative. Please spend some time devising your own answers.

- *"Why had the wind and weather favored her?" ("The Legend of the Sparrow," see page 36.)*

- *"What voices heard you in the holy place?" ("The Mountains of the Lord")*

- *"Who walked these streets of night?" ("The Uninvited")*

- *"Whom do I love, O God, when I love thee?" ("Repairer of Fences," see page 53.)*

- *"Who would believe me if I said that grace / devised this lodging in a lowly place?" ("The Rock Too High for Me")*

- *"How can a man in love sit and stare?" ("I Would Define My Love")*

- *"...[I]s not pure fact a fullness?" ("Siesta in Color")*

- *"How does one hush one's house...?" ("The House at Rest," see page 46.)*

- *"And then I thought: where truly do we go?"* *("The Terminal")*

- *"Yet who am I to minimize the worth / of what a stump is likely to bring forth?"* *("There Shall Come Forth a Shoot")*

Unable to refrain, I have also provided my own responses.

1) "Why had the wind and weather favored her?" Some people are born with a silver spoon in their mouth. Others contact silver or gold only once or twice on the journey; still others, never. So what's the explanation for being "favored," "graced"? Reasons range from haphazard circumstance to the gratuity of God. Whatever the explanation, the wind and weather can sometimes be friendly and elicit joy in the heart. Telling this to King Lear will seem ludicrous; proposing this truth to a bird in ecstatic flight will be well received.

2) "What voices heard you in the holy place?"

the voice of the owl   uttering wisdom
the voice of the hawk   crying death
the voice of the finch   whispering joy
the voice of the jay   screaming commands
the voice of the crow   barking a dirge

and the holy place was my backyard

3) "Who walked these streets of night?" Some folks walk the streets of day, others the streets of night. When the sun sets, people of means enter their homes, sit down for a meal, find comfort in their place of security. With

the closing of day, others have nowhere to go. The streets become (continue to be) their home with their hidden dangers and perpetual violence. Fear dominates the darkness and anguish burdens the heart. Some of these night street-walkers are children abandoned by parents, elderly who have experienced life as a failure, men and women who are simply lost. But, strange to say, in the dark night of the streets a divine light flickers and sends forth a ray of hope.

4) "Whom do I love, O God, when I love thee?" Saint Augustine cries out in his *Confessions* that he loved too late a God ever ancient, ever new. Whether our love is late or earlier, we must ponder the question of the nature of God. Love calls for knowledge. Knowledge comes with revelation. For Christians, the God loved is revealed in Jesus, a child born in poverty, an itinerant preacher, a crucified Lord, a risen Christ. The God we love is found in the historical Jesus and in his Mystical Body.

5) "Who would believe me if I said that grace / devised this lodging in a lowly place?" Providence is a profound mystery. The ways of God are so different from our own. We would eliminate suffering and death; God uses these for new life. We choose the first and exalted places; God selects the last and lowly. We seek happiness in fulfilling our needs; God guides us toward service and sacrifice to bring peace to our souls. People find it hard to believe that God's geography is the desert and darkness, that these are the dwelling places of grace.

6) "How can a man in love sit and stare?" Love is active. An affinity felt deep within devises ways to union, to bonding. No longer is solitude acceptable. A word must be spoken, a hand touched, gifts given. Love

overflows into an energy that demands expression. Love is essentially incarnational. Platonic lovers may sit and stare but all others are engaged in passionate activities that show concern.

7) "...[I]s not pure fact a fullness?" Years ago I heard the statement in a lecture: "Experiences unreflected upon dehumanize." Later I heard another question, which might be put this way: "Experience is sufficient unto itself; why ask for meaning?" We humans straddle two worlds: the immediacy of fact and the search for meaning. Fortunately, we can have it both ways. The caution is simply not to seek meaning too fast. The caution is to taste the fact to the full and let the meaning come when it will.

8) "How does one hush one's house...?" Grand Central Station in New York is a busy place. Rare are the times it is hushed. Our interior is often no less noisy. Thoughts and memories and fears and anxieties stream through at will, knocking over table and chair, causing general chaos. What can bring us peace and quiet, what can hush our houses? One answer is virtue. Habitually doing what is right brings peace. Another answer is to welcome a guest, the Spirit of peace, who puts all in order.

9) "And then I thought: where truly do we go?" "*Quo vadis?* Where are you going?" We can answer that quite easily in terms of our short jaunts: to the store, down by the lake, over to Grandma's, to Hawaii. But the larger "where" question awaits us all: to the grave—and beyond? Christian faith states that there are only two final destinations: We are either going to heaven (union with God and the saints) or bound for hell (separation from God and others). There may be a brief stop in

purgatory. The atheist and the agnostic are stuck with the grave. Some eastern religions have us circle back for another go at it. "Where truly do we go?" haunts the human spirit.

10) "Yet who am I to minimize the worth / of what a stump is likely to bring forth?" While cutting out balsam fir trees for a Christmas tree sale, I noted a stump from last year's harvesting. A small bud was emerging from the barren piece of wood and I knew, with proper nurturing and trimming, another tree would flower into gentle beauty. Just a year ago the stump had lost its hard-earned growth. Now new life was breaking forth out of the darkness of death. How dare I minimize the power of nature?

Resources

Books

Kappes, C.S.T., Marianne. *Track of the Mystic: The Spirituality of Jessica Powers*. Kansas City, Mo.: Sheed & Ward, 1994.

Leckey, Dolores. *Winter Music: A Life of Jessica Powers*. Kansas City, Mo.: Sheed & Ward, 1992.

Morneau, Robert F. Morneau. *Mantras From a Poet: Jessica Powers*. Kansas City, Mo.: Sheed & Ward, 1991.

Selected Poetry of Jessica Powers. Edited by Regina Siegfried and Robert Morneau. Kansas City, Mo.: Sheed & Ward, 1989.

Audiocassettes

Merton, Thomas. *Poetry and Religious Experience*. Kansas City, Mo.: Credence Cassettes, 1995.

Morneau, Bishop Robert F. *Jessica Powers: Landscapes of the Sacred*. Staten Island, N.Y.: Alba House Cassettes, 1991.